# THE POWER OF MANIFESTATION

## UNLOCKING THE PATH

## FROM THOUGHT TO REALITY

Awaken Your Inner Creator—Align Your Energy, Shape Your Destiny

**SHREE SHAMBAV**

THE POWER OF MANIFESTATION

UNLOCKING THE PATH FROM THOUGHT TO REALITY

Shree Shambav

Published by Shree Shambav, Tamil Nadu, India
Shree Shambav Ink & Imagination "Where Words Breathe and Imagination Soars"
All Rights Reserved

First Edition, 2025

Copyright © 2025, Muniswamy Rajakumar

All rights reserved. No part of this publication may be reproduced, distributed, or transmitted in any form or by any means, including photocopying, recording, or other electronic or mechanical methods, without the author's prior written permission. It is illegal to copy this book, post it to a website, or distribute it by any other means without permission.

The request for permission should be addressed to the author.

ISBN: 978-93-343-1353-6

Email: shreeshambav@gmail.com

Web: www.shambav.org

# DEDICATION

"Isavasyam idam sarvam yat kim ca jagatyam jagat, tena tyaktena bhunjitha, ma gridhah kasyasvid dhanam"

To the Almighty,

the Divine Masters,

the family who listens,

and my parents who see –

your presence shapes the pages of my life's journey.

"Isavasyam idam sarvam yat kim ca jagatyam jagat"

*Meaning: "God encompasses everything you perceive, see, or touch with your sense organs."*

# DISCLAIMER

The Power of Manifestation: Unlocking the Path from Thought to Reality

*Awaken Your Inner Creator—Align Your Energy, Shape Your Destiny*

This book is more than a guide—it's a heartfelt invitation to rediscover the creative force that has always lived within you.

It unveils the sacred dance between thought, belief, emotion, and the universe, showing how your inner world sculpts your outer life. Combining ancient wisdom, modern science, and soulful reflection, this book offers a practical and profound journey into conscious manifestation. Whether you're seeking clarity, purpose, abundance, or deep emotional alignment, this is your roadmap to becoming the architect of your own destiny.

**Why You Should Read This Book**

- To understand how your thoughts and emotions shape your reality.
- To break free from limiting beliefs and embrace empowered, conscious living.
- To explore the synergy of science, spirituality, and self-mastery in simple, actionable steps.

- To learn real-world tools for manifesting love, health, wealth, and purpose.

- Because manifestation isn't magic—it's the art of living with intention, alignment, and awareness.

- This book isn't about blind optimism—it's about awakening your ability to create a life that reflects your deepest truth.

The practices and principles shared are based on personal experiences, research, and spiritual insights and are meant to support readers in their personal growth journey. Individual results may vary, as manifestation is influenced by a wide range of personal beliefs, intentions, actions, and circumstances.

The author and publisher make no guarantees of specific outcomes and are not liable for any actions taken or not taken based on the contents of this book. Always trust your own judgment and seek professional advice where appropriate.

*Note - If any part of the book, in any sequence, hurts the reader's sentiments, it would be just out of a sheer accident, not intentional*

# EPIGRAM

## THE POWER OF MANIFESTATION

"The universe does not grant wishes to those who wait—it responds to those who align. Thoughts ignite, emotions shape, and actions anchor the invisible into reality."

– Shree Shambav

# THE POWER OF MANIFESTATION

## UNLOCKING THE PATH

## FROM THOUGHT TO REALITY

### Shree Shambav

**Shree Shambav is a 36x best-selling author renowned for his transformative works in personal development and spiritual growth.**

# Dear Cherished Readers

Dear Cherished Readers,

As I embark on this new literary voyage, my heart swells with profound gratitude and an overwhelming sense of connection. With deep emotion, I extend my heartfelt appreciation to each of you who has joined me on this journey.

With sincere warmth, I invite you to revisit the steps we have taken together through the pages of my earlier works. Our odyssey began with "Journey of Soul - Karma," a book that marked my first foray into the world of words and a testament to the raw passion that ignited my writing adventure.

The subsequent chapters of our shared journey unfolded through the enchanting tapestry of the *"Twenty + One"* series. With each page turned, it felt as though a brushstroke was added to the canvas of our collective imagination—stories and sentiments woven to echo within the quiet corners of your heart. These weren't just words; they were invitations to feel, to reflect, and to remember what truly matters.

And how can I not cherish the transformative path we walked together through the *"Life Changing Journey—Inspirational Quotes Series?"* Day by day, quote by quote, we ventured inward—into spaces often overlooked—to find wisdom in simplicity and light in life's shadows. Each reflection was offered as a gentle whisper of hope, a spark meant to uplift, inspire, and remind us that even in silence, the soul speaks.

The release of "Death - Light of Life and the Shadow of Death" promises to shed new light on the timeless mystery of death. Similarly, "Unleashing the Incredible Potential of Programming with Python - Optimum - PYTHON: Ultimate Guide for Beginners Series I" is poised to empower readers with newfound knowledge.

In addition, my technical book, OPTIMUM Python Series II - Exploring Data Structures and Algorithms, delves into advanced concepts in Python programming, offering a comprehensive guide for those seeking to deepen their understanding.

OPTIMUM – Python Power Series III is your essential guide to mastering the most powerful Python libraries for data science. From data manipulation and visualisation to machine learning, this book empowers you with practical tools to solve real-world challenges. Unleash your potential and transform the way you work with data.

Shree Shambav expands his artistic repertoire with *"Whispers of Eternity: 150 Plus - A Symphony of Soulful Verses,"* a heartfelt exploration of the human experience. Alongside this, his *"Whispers of the Soul: A Journey Through Haiku"* distils profound insights into poignant verses. Together, these works showcase his versatility and mastery of soulful expression, inviting readers on a journey of self-discovery. Through his poetry, he weaves a rich tapestry of emotion that resonates deeply with the heart.

Shree Shambav's latest works—*Learn to Love Yourself: A Journey of Discovering Inner Beauty and Strength Through 10 Transformative Rules, The Power of Letting Go: Embrace Freedom and Happiness, A Journey of Lasting Peace*—are true treasures of self-discovery, *The Entitlement Trap: Get Over It, Get On, Whispers of a Dying Soul: Unspoken Regrets and Unlived Dreams, Whispers of Silence - Unlocking Inner Power through Stillness, The Power of Words: Transforming Speech, Transforming Lives, The Art of Intentional Living: Minimalism for a Life of Purpose, Awakening the Infinite:The Power of Consciousness in Transforming Life, Beyond the Veil: A Journey Through Life After Death series, Bonds Beyond Blood - Where love builds bridges, and bonds defy blood.,* and *A Journey into Spiritual Maturity - 12 Golden Rules for Inner Transformation.*

In addition to these works, Shree Shambav has recently ventured into astrology with the release of Astrology Unveiled – Foundations of Ancient Wisdom Series I to VI, expanding into the realm of metaphysics. These books explore the foundational principles of Vedic astrology, offering readers a rich and practical understanding of this ancient wisdom.

Your unwavering support, enthusiasm to immerse yourself in my writings, and readiness to embark on these journeys with me have been my greatest sources of inspiration. Your input has been a beacon guiding me through the creation process, moulding these stories into containers of passion, emotion, knowledge, and resonance.

As I unveil this new narrative before you, know that your presence, insights, and shared moments have been my companions. The path we have walked together is etched in the annals of my creative evolution, and it's an honour beyond words to have you by my side once more.

Here's to the readers who have illuminated my path with their presence, who have embraced my stories with open hearts, and who have woven themselves into the very fabric of my literary world. Our journey has been a symbiotic dance of writer and reader, a harmony of souls brought together by the magic of storytelling.

With a heart brimming with appreciation and eyes glistening with anticipation, I extend my deepest gratitude for your unwavering support. Thank you for the memories, the shared emotions, and the countless hours spent in the worlds we've crafted together. As we step into this new adventure, let's continue to explore, feel, and discover the boundless horizons that words can unveil.

Warmly,

Shree Shambav

THE POWER OF MANIFESTATION

# Suggested Reads

FROM BEST-SELLING AUTHOR

# Endorsements

"The Power of Manifestation is more than just a book—it's an awakening. Shree Shambav beautifully weaves ancient wisdom with modern science, offering not just theories but a practical guide for anyone yearning to turn their inner visions into lived reality. This book reminds us that manifestation is not wishful thinking, but a sacred, conscious collaboration with the universe. If you've ever felt the quiet ache for a life aligned with your heart's deepest desires—this book is your map."

— Uma Devi, Entrepreunuer

# About the Author

Shree Shambav is an internationally acclaimed best-selling author, inspirational speaker, artist, philanthropist, life coach, and entrepreneur. A world record holder, his deep passion for music led him to create soul-stirring albums, drawing inspiration from his celebrated poetry collection, Whispers of Eternity. His profound insights have sparked deep personal transformations, guiding countless individuals toward self-discovery, purposeful living, and authenticity.

With an extraordinary ability to unlock human potential, Shree empowers individuals to break through limitations and embrace their highest selves. His writings, lectures, and compassionate guidance continue to uplift lives, fostering resilience, mindfulness, and personal growth.

Shree Shambav is a 35x best-selling author celebrated for his profound contributions to personal development and spiritual growth.

Shree Shambav's literary journey took flight with the celebrated Journey of Soul - Karma, where he delved into the depths of human experience to unveil profound insights. Garnering recognition through multiple literature awards, his repertoire includes esteemed works, such as the Twenty + One Series, and the enlightening Life Changing Journey – Inspirational Quotes series.

As a distinguished alumnus of the Indian Institute of Management and the National Institute of Technology, Shree Shambav brings a wealth of corporate acumen from his tenure in multinational corporations. His most recent publications, including Unveiling the Enigma, Death - Light of Life and the Shadow of Death and Optimum – Power Python Series I, Series II and Series III, demonstrate his mastery of both the literary and technical spheres.

Shree Shambav expands his artistic repertoire with "*Whispers of Eternity: 150 Plus - A Symphony of Soulful Verses*," a heartfelt exploration of the human experience. Alongside this, his "*Whispers of the Soul: A Journey Through Haiku*" distils profound insights into poignant verses. Together, these works showcase his versatility and mastery of soulful expression, inviting readers on a journey of self-discovery. Through his poetry, he weaves a rich tapestry of emotion that resonates deeply with the heart.

Shree Shambav's latest works—*Learn to Love Yourself: A Journey of Discovering Inner Beauty and Strength Through 10 Transformative*

*Rules, The Power of Letting Go: Embrace Freedom and Happiness, A Journey of Lasting Peace*—are true treasures of self-discovery, *The Entitlement Trap: Get Over It, Get On, Whispers of a Dying Soul: Unspoken Regrets and Unlived Dreams, Whispers of Silence - Unlocking Inner Power through Stillness, The Power of Words: Transforming Speech, Transforming Lives, The Art of Intentional Living: Minimalism for a Life of Purpose, Awakening the Infinite: The Power of Consciousness in Transforming Life, Beyond the Veil: A Journey Through Life After Death series, Bonds Beyond Blood - Where love builds bridges, and bonds defy blood.*, and *A Journey into Spiritual Maturity - 12 Golden Rules for Inner Transformation.*

In addition to these works, Shree Shambav has recently ventured into astrology with the release of Astrology Unveiled – Foundations of Ancient Wisdom Series I to VI, expanding into the realm of metaphysics. These books explore the foundational principles of Vedic astrology, offering readers a rich and practical understanding of this ancient wisdom.

Shree Shambav established the Ayur Rakshita Foundation, which is dedicated to promoting boundless growth, universal fraternity, and environmental protection. The charity helps diverse communities while working for societal progress.

To learn more about Shree Shambav and his works, visit his website at www.shambav.org. For information about the Ayur Rakshita Foundation and its initiatives, visit www.shambav-ayurrakshita.org.

Let's Follow him on Social Media: **@shreeshambav**

Main: https://linktr.ee/shreeshambav

Website: https://www.shambav.org/

# SHREE SHAMBAV

LinkedIn: https://www.linkedin.com/in/shreeshambav/

Blog: https://blog.shambav.org/

Instagram: https://www.instagram.com/shreeshambav/

YouTube: https://www.youtube.com/@shreeshambav

Amazon: https://www.amazon.com/author/shreeshambav

Goodreads: https://www.goodreads.com/author/show/22367436.Shree_Shambav

# PREFACE

**Awaken Your Inner Creator—Align Your Energy, Shape Your Destiny**

There comes a moment in every life—quiet, unassuming, but profound—when you pause and wonder: *Is this all there is?*

Not the life you've inherited, not the circumstances you've adapted to, but the deeper life—life-the one whispered to you in your dreams, felt in the silence between thoughts, and glimpsed in fleeting moments of awe.

This book is born from that sacred pause.

**Manifestation is not a modern trend.** It is not an act of wishing hard enough or reciting affirmations until the universe listens. It is not about bending reality to suit your ego, but rather learning the delicate art of aligning yourself with the rhythm of existence—and becoming the co-architect of your own reality.

You are not here by accident. You are both a participant and a creator in this unfolding universe, bound by unseen laws as old as time, yet free to choose how you dance within them. This book is designed to guide you from **curiosity to conscious creation**—to help you peel back the veil between thought and reality, so you can awaken the inner creator you were always meant to be.

Whether you wish to attract abundance, deepen relationships, heal emotionally or physically, or rediscover a long-lost sense of purpose, the journey begins not in the world outside, but within the energy that shapes it.

You hold the power to shift your reality not by force, but through alignment—by learning the language of the universe: thought, emotion, intention, and action woven in harmony.

**The chapters that follow are your compass.** From the ancient truths that explain the architecture of reality to the practices that anchor manifestation in daily life, this book will offer not only understanding but practical tools for you to walk this path with clarity, courage, and love.

You do not have to be perfect to manifest a beautiful life. You only have to be awake, willing, and aligned.

This is your invitation to remember that you are more than a drop in the ocean.

You are the ocean, learning to move as a wave.

**Welcome to The Power of Manifestation.**

Let's begin.

With gratitude and encouragement,

Shree Shambav

# INTRODUCTION

**The Hidden Force Within**

Have you ever stood under a starlit sky, gazed into the quiet infinity, and felt—if only for a fleeting moment—that life is more than random chance? That somehow, your thoughts, feelings, and desires are part of a conversation much older and grander than yourself?

That feeling is not imagination.

It's a quiet remembrance of truth.

At the heart of this book is that very truth: **manifestation is not magic, it is the natural unfolding of creation through you**—a force as real as gravity, as intimate as breath, and as powerful as the universe itself.

From the day you were born, whether you realised it or not, you've been manifesting. Your beliefs shaped your choices, your emotions sculpted your days, and your thoughts whispered to reality like artists to blank canvases. Life was not happening to you. Life was happening *through* you.

But for many, this sacred power lies dormant, tangled in old fears, limiting beliefs, and forgotten dreams. The world often teaches us to chase and control, to struggle and force. It rarely teaches us to align. And yet, true manifestation begins with one profound realisation:

**You are already connected to everything you seek.**

This book is not here to sell you wishful thinking. It is not here to promise quick fixes or the illusion of instant success. Instead, it is here to help you remember the quiet, empowering truth that the world you experience is a mirror, and you are both the seer and the artist.

When you shift your inner world, the outer world cannot help but follow.

When you release resistance and align your thoughts, emotions, and actions, the universe responds not out of obligation, but out of natural law.

Whether you are here to call in love, health, abundance, peace, or purpose, this journey will lead you home. Home to your own creative essence. Home to the deep trust that you were never meant to struggle alone. Home to the understanding that manifestation is not reserved for the few but for every soul brave enough to believe, align, and act.

So this is where your journey begins—with humility, with wonder, and with an open heart. The chapters ahead are more than teachings; they are invitations to rewrite the story of your life.

Because the greatest truth of all is this:

**The power you seek has always been within you.**

*It is time to remember.*
*It is time to awaken.*
*It is time to manifest.*

Let the journey begin.

With warmth and sincerity,

Shree Shambav

# PROLOGUE

**The Silent Art of Becoming**

There is a quiet force that shapes the world—and it does so without noise, without fame, and without applause. It is older than time, subtler than breath, and more powerful than any earthly possession. You've known it since the day you first dreamed of a future. You've felt its stirrings in the quiet spaces between hope and doubt, success and surrender.

This force is a **manifestation**.

It is not a new-age trend, nor is it wishful thinking wrapped in modern language. Manifestation is the ancient, unspoken art of weaving thoughts, emotions, and intentions into the fabric of reality. Whether you've realised it or not, you have always been manifesting—through your beliefs, your choices, your feelings, and the quiet stories you tell yourself about who you are and what you deserve.

The world you experience is not random. It is a mirror, reflecting not your wishes, but your inner alignment.

This book is not written to teach you how to control life, for life was never meant to be controlled. It was meant to be co-created. You are both the artist and the canvas, both the seed and the bloom. When you align your mind, heart, and energy with truth, the world does not simply change around you—it changes through you.

In these pages, you will journey beyond the surface of material desires into the depths of conscious creation. You will come to see that manifestation is not about forcing reality to bend to your will, but about harmonising your inner world so the universe meets you with grace and abundance.

This is a return to your natural power.

A homecoming to your limitless potential.

A gentle reminder that the world you long for—is longing for you, too.

The power to shape your destiny has always been within you.

Now, it's time to remember.

# CONTENTS

DEDICATION ................................................................... iii
DISCLAIMER ..................................................................... v
EPIGRAM ........................................................................ vii
Dear Cherished Readers ................................................... xi
Suggested Reads ............................................................. xv
Endorsements ................................................................ xvii
About the Author ............................................................ xix
PREFACE ....................................................................... xxiii
INTRODUCTION ............................................................. xxv
PROLOGUE ................................................................... xxix
CONTENTS .................................................................... xxxi
At Kumbhariyur ................................................................. 1
   Whispers of the Mist ..................................................... 1
PART ONE ........................................................................ 1
   The Foundations of Manifestation ................................. 1
CHAPTER I ........................................................................ 1
   The Invisible Sculptor of Reality ................................... 1
CHAPTER II ..................................................................... 13
   The Language of the Universe ..................................... 13
CHAPTER III .................................................................... 29
   The Divine Dialogue .................................................... 29

## CHAPTER IV ............ 45
How Entanglement Fuels Manifestation ............ 45

## PART TWO ............ 69
Reprogramming the Self ............ 69

## CHAPTER V ............ 71
The Inner Compass ............ 71

## CHAPTER VI ............ 87
The Invisible Thread ............ 87

## CHAPTER VII ............ 105
The Soul's Cosmic Library ............ 105

## CHAPTER VIII ............ 127
The Eternal Dance ............ 127

## CHAPTER IX ............ 145
The Heart's Role in Manifestation ............ 145

## PART THREE ............ 163
Manifestation in Action ............ 163

## CHAPTER X ............ 165
How to Manifest Consciously ............ 165

## CHAPTER XI ............ 177
The Sacred Practices of Manifestation ............ 177

## PART FOUR ............ 195
Manifestation in Everyday Life ............ 195

## CHAPTER XII ............ 197
Manifestation ............ 197

**PART FIVE** .................................................................. 221
   The Manifestor's Lifestyle ............................................... 221
**CHAPTER XIII** ............................................................. 223
   Living as a Manifestor ..................................................... 223
**WRAP UP** ................................................................... 237
   Becoming the Architect of Your Destiny ....................... 237
**The Garden Within** ........................................................ 247
**Life Coach and Philanthropist** .......................................... 251
**TESTIMONIALS** ............................................................ 253
**ACKNOWLEDGEMENTS** ................................................ 261

# At Kumbhariyur
## Whispers of the Mist

*"Every thought is a seed, planted in the soil of the universe. Nurtured by emotion, it grows into the reality you call your life."*

- Shree Shambav

The morning in Kumbhariyur unfolded like a sacred hymn—the sky painted in muted hues, the hills wrapped in a silken shawl of fog, and the earth exhaling the chill of the night in slow, fragrant breaths. It wasn't just a village awakening—it was life, pausing to bow in reverence before beginning anew.

The trees stood still as if listening, the leaves barely stirring in the hush. In this timeless cradle of nature, there was a silence so deep that it echoed. The birds, the frogs, even the wind seemed to know—something was sacred here.

Abhilasha stood apart, not out of pride, but out of presence. She faced the east where dawn, like a hesitant artist, had begun brushing the horizon with gold. Her breath moved in rhythm with the earth's silence. Others bustled to keep warm, tugging shawls tighter and rubbing their hands, but she lingered, her spirit caught in the whisper between the light and the mist.

Then, Akshaya's voice, warm and grounding, cut through the hush, "Guruji is planning to have the morning session under this grand tree…"

Apeksha's smile lingered as her gaze lifted toward the banyan's sweeping canopy. The others turned to her with curiosity.

Nita nudged her gently. "Apeksha, why do you always smile around this tree?"

Apeksha chuckled softly. "It's silly, but unforgettable. Years ago, during our very first retreat here, I came early one morning to sit under this tree. I was feeling… lost, unsure of everything—my work, my relationships, even my purpose. I just wanted clarity. I sat right there," she pointed to the patch of earth where the roots curled like wise old fingers, "and I started crying quietly."

The group fell silent, the rustling leaves above seeming to lean in closer.

"I didn't notice anyone had arrived," she continued, "but after a few minutes, I heard a voice. It was Guruji. He didn't ask me what was wrong. He just sat beside me and said, 'Sometimes the soul doesn't need answers. It just needs to be held by silence.' We sat there… not talking, not solving—just breathing."

Her voice softened as emotion caught in her throat.

"And then…" she laughed, wiping a corner of her eye, "as if the tree itself wanted to comfort me, a gentle breeze blew, and a whole shower of dry leaves came tumbling down—right into Guruji's teacup! He looked at me, smiled with that peaceful face of his, and said, 'Even the tree knows when it's time to release.'"

Everyone burst into laughter, the image vivid in their minds.

Abhilasha placed a gentle hand on the tree's bark. "So the tree remembered."

"Yes," Apeksha whispered. "And so did I."

They stood quietly for a moment, sipping the warm tea someone had brought from the cottage, the aroma grounding them in the present while the story drifted through the air like a fragrant memory.

Akanksh stepped closer to the base of the tree and sat cross-legged, inviting the others with a nod.

Kiran glanced at his watch, then at the sky. "Time to get ready for today's session," he said, but even that reminder felt poetic.

They walked slowly, not to reach—but to feel. With every step, the village whispered to them that life isn't always about the pace, but the presence.

By the time they gathered beneath the grand banyan tree, the world had shifted. The sun had climbed just enough. The wind hummed a sacred note. And then, Guruji appeared—his smile deep, his steps steady.

He sat on his asana with a gentle *Atma Namaste*, eyes briefly closing, drawing them all into his stillness. Then, without a word, he opened his gaze and looked at them as if he could see not their faces, but their essence.

*Abhilasha's voice, tender yet fierce, broke the silence. "Guruji, what if every thought, emotion, and belief we hold is already influencing the reality we live in—are we aware of the role we play in shaping our life?"*

Guruji spoke—not with the urgency of answers, but with the depth of remembrance.

"Abhilasha," he said, his voice carrying the warmth of the rising sun, "do you see this banyan tree?"

She nodded.

"This tree," he began, "once lived as a thought inside a seed. A tiny, almost invisible idea of life, resting quietly beneath the soil. It had no voice, no movement, no evidence of greatness. But it held the memory of forests. The potential of shade, of shelter, of serenity. It did not question how or when—it simply *aligned* with its nature. And slowly, with light and darkness, storms and sun, it became this magnificent being you see now."

He paused. The wind rustled through the leaves as if affirming his words.

"Now imagine," he continued, "if that seed had doubted its own nature. What if it feared its growth? Or believed it wasn't worthy of sunlight? Would this tree still be standing here, holding us in its embrace?"

Abhilasha's eyes glistened.

"Our thoughts," Guruji said, "are like seeds. Our emotions, the waters that nourish them. Our beliefs, the sunlight—or the shadow—they grow under. Every single moment, we are planting something into the soil of our reality. And whether we are conscious of it or not, life is growing in the image of those seeds."

He turned gently to the others, who now sat in stillness—caught in the pull of memory and insight.

"There was a time," he said, "when I too lived by default. Letting the storms of the world dictate my seasons. Until one day, I realised the garden I was walking through was my own making—every thorn, every flower. And that day… I chose to become a gardener."

He looked back at Abhilasha.

"So yes. Every thought, every feeling, every belief you cradle is already sculpting your tomorrow. And awareness is not just the first step—it is the light that allows us to see the seeds in our hands. When you are aware, you are no longer a wanderer in the wilderness. You are a weaver of destiny."

A moment of stillness followed, heavy and sacred.

And then—a soft breath of wind stirred the leaves above them, and a single golden leaf drifted gently down, landing beside Abhilasha. She picked it up delicately, tracing its edges.

Guruji smiled. "Even the tree has answered."

The group sat in reverent quiet, hearts heavy with meaning and light with understanding. In that moment, the banyan was no longer just a tree—it was a mirror, a memory, a mentor. And the morning had shifted, imperceptibly but irreversibly.

They were no longer just seekers gathered in the shade. They were sowers of light.

The question settled like a stone dropped into a still pond—ripples spreading wide, disturbing nothing, yet touching everything.

*Akanksh's gaze was steady, but there was something searching in his eyes. "Guruji," he asked, "why has manifestation been described as both a spiritual truth and a scientific curiosity throughout history—what hidden knowledge have we overlooked in our modern lives?"*

Guruji sat motionless for a moment. Only the rustle of leaves overhead and the soft murmur of morning winds filled the space. He looked at Akanksh, not with an answer, but with a depth that could only come from having once stood in that same space of wondering.

"Akanksh," he began gently, "do you remember the story of the sculptor who wandered into the forest, burdened by a block of stone too large for his cart?"

Akanksh nodded faintly, intrigued.

"This sculptor had travelled far in search of the perfect stone. Not for wealth, not for fame—but to carve a statue of the divine, the embodiment of truth he had seen only in dreams. But when he finally found the stone, it was far too heavy, too rough, and too imperfect. So he left it behind and continued searching, hoping for something more refined.

Years passed. Seasons changed. And one day, weary and disappointed, he returned to the same forest—only to find that another had taken that very block and carved from it a form so breathtaking, so filled with presence, that it radiated stillness and power. It wasn't perfection that the sculptor had missed—it was the willingness to see through the stone."

Guruji paused.

"Manifestation," he continued, "is like that block of stone. It is always present—rough, silent, unnoticed. But only those with the eyes of devotion and the hands of awareness can sculpt from it something sacred."

The group sat quietly, breathing in the meaning.

"You see, Akanksh," Guruji said, "manifestation is not a modern invention, nor a mystical delusion. It is the very blueprint of existence. The ancient seers called it *tapasya*, the yogis called it *sankalpa*, and the sages of the Vedas spoke of *ritam*—the cosmic order that responds to inner alignment. In the East, they saw it as a divine co-creation. In the West, modern science now calls it quantum entanglement, the observer effect, or neuroplasticity. But it is the same thread, described in different tongues."

He leaned forward slightly.

"The truth is—we are not just flesh and bone. We are consciousness wrapped in memory, intention wrapped in energy. Our thoughts are not idle; they are frequencies. Our emotions are not fleeting; they are magnetic fields. Every belief is like a prism—bending light in a way that colours our reality."

Guruji's voice softened.

"In our modern lives, distracted by screens and schedules, we have forgotten the sacred pause. We've abandoned silence for stimulation. We want instant results, but manifestation is not a vending machine—it is a seed. And seeds need time, trust, and tending."

He turned his gaze skyward, through the branches of the banyan that framed the rising sun.

"We overlook the space between," he said. "The invisible. The subtle. But it is in the invisible where the real power lives. The soil does not show you the roots, yet the roots are what hold the tree."

Akanksh's eyes shimmered—not with tears, but with something deeper: remembrance.

Guruji smiled gently. "To manifest is not to force. It is to align. To become so whole, so true within yourself, that the universe cannot help but reflect you. That is the hidden knowledge: you are not separate from creation. You are a living instrument of it."

The banyan leaves rustled as a breeze swept through, cool and fragrant.

Guruji looked around and added, "We are not here to control the universe. We are here to dance with it. And every thought, every breath, every belief... is a step in that sacred choreography."

The silence that followed wasn't empty—it was full. Full of realisation, of stillness, of unseen truth rising to the surface.

Akanksh closed his eyes for a brief moment, breathing in deeply, as if something dormant within him had been stirred awake. When he opened them, he looked not at Guruji—but at the banyan, the sky, the soil, and himself, with new eyes.

Akshatha's voice carried a stillness, as if the question had formed not just in her mind, but had risen gently from somewhere deep within her soul.

*"Guruji,"* she asked, *"if the universe is an intelligent and responsive force, how would our intentions, choices, and actions change from today onward?"*

A quiet hush fell over the group again, like the Earth itself had leaned in to listen.

Guruji looked toward her, his eyes steady but kind—like the river that watches mountains crumble with time, but never rushes their fall.

He took a long breath before speaking.

"Akshatha," he said softly, "have you ever walked through a field of sunflowers just before sunset?"

She nodded slowly, intrigued.

"There's something extraordinary that happens there," Guruji began. "No matter where you stand in the field, every single sunflower turns toward the sun, following its arc through the sky. Not out of fear. Not out of doubt. But from a silent, innate intelligence. A knowing that the source of life is worthy of their full attention."

He paused, letting the imagery take root.

"Now imagine," he continued, "if we, too, recognised the universe as that sun—an aware, living force of light—and if we aligned our inner compass not toward fear or survival, but toward that same radiant intelligence… how differently would we live?"

Akshatha's eyes softened, listening not only with her ears, but with her breath.

"You see, most people live as though life is random," Guruji continued. "They act out of habit, speak without awareness, and carry intentions shaped by old wounds, not wisdom. But the moment you truly *know*—not just believe—that the universe is listening… that it responds not to your desperation, but to your vibration… everything changes."

He leaned slightly forward.

"Suddenly, every intention becomes sacred. Not just the big ones, like building a home or finding love, but even the quiet ones—how you greet a stranger, how you speak to yourself, how you walk through this Earth."

A light wind rustled the leaves above them.

"Imagine if the wind were your witness, the trees your teachers, the stars your silent allies. If your choices were not based on convenience, but on consciousness—how would that change how you spend your time, how you speak your truth, how you treat your body, your relationships, your gifts?"

Guruji's eyes searched Akshatha's with depth.

"When you live as if the universe is alive—truly alive—your actions stop being mechanical. Your thoughts are no longer noise; they become offerings. Your life stops being a sequence of reactions and begins to bloom into a deliberate creation. Like a gardener who doesn't just scatter seeds, but whispers to the soil."

The group sat spellbound, their hearts drawn inward.

"And here's the most beautiful part," Guruji said, his voice like sunlight through cloud. "The moment you begin treating the universe as conscious… it reveals its consciousness to you.

Not always in dramatic miracles, but in subtle synchronicities—a book that finds you, a stranger who speaks your unspoken thought, a sudden clarity that emerges from silence. These are not coincidences; they are conversations."

He looked around slowly, his gaze resting briefly on each face.

"So, Akshatha," he said, returning to her, "if you were to live each day from this awareness—from this sacred reverence—that the universe is not just a backdrop, but a beloved co-creator… You would not merely survive this life. You would *dance* with it."

Akshatha felt her heart swell, not with emotion alone, but with a gentle awakening—as if something within her had heard its name spoken for the first time.

Guruji closed his eyes briefly, then opened them again.

"From today onward, may your intentions be clear, your choices be conscious, and your actions be aligned with love. That is the beginning of living not as a lost traveller… but as a luminous creator."

The leaves above them whispered in a hushed rhythm, the kind only the oldest trees know. Apeksha sat with her hands resting softly on her knees, her eyes lifted toward Guruji. In her voice was both innocence and courage.

*"Guruji," she said, her tone delicate but firm, "are we willing to shift from being a passive dreamer to an active creator of our own reality—and what beliefs or doubts must we release to begin?"*

The question hovered in the space between them, a sacred ember waiting to be tended.

Guruji looked at her, and then at the circle gathered under the sacred banyan. His gaze lingered for a moment longer on each face, as though he could see the dreamer and the doubter within them all.

He inhaled slowly, as if drawing breath not just from the air, but from the very essence of the Earth beneath them.

"Apeksha," he began gently, "let me tell you a story."

He reached for a small stone beside him, weathered and smooth, and placed it in his palm.

"Many years ago, in a village not far from here, lived a potter named Vedan. Every day, Vedan shaped clay into vessels—cups, lamps, urns—his hands worn, his back bent, but his spirit quietly steady."

Guruji's fingers mimed the shape of a wheel turning.

"One day, a traveller came to him and asked, 'Vedan, how do you shape such perfect pots?' And Vedan replied, 'I don't shape the clay. I shape the space *within* it. The clay is only the boundary—what matters is the emptiness I'm preparing for.'"

The group fell still.

"This," Guruji continued, "is the art of shifting from dreaming to creating. Most people focus only on the clay—on the external world, the appearances, the noise. But the true creator tends to the *space* within—the beliefs, emotions, doubts, and visions that form the unseen architecture of reality."

He turned to Apeksha.

"To become an active creator, you must first acknowledge that you are already dreaming—always dreaming. But a passive dreamer lets life happen *to* them. They say, 'I wish', 'I hope', 'If only'. Their dreams stay locked in the attic of someday."

Apeksha nodded, her eyes already shimmering with something ancient and tender.

"But an active creator," Guruji said, "asks a different question: 'What must I *let go* of to let my dream through?'"

He drew a slow circle in the dirt with his finger.

"We hold on to things that do not serve us: the belief that we are not enough, the fear of judgment, the idea that we must first suffer to deserve joy. These are not truths. These are just heavy clothes we forgot we were wearing."

He looked back at the stone in his hand.

"To create is to unclench. To release. You cannot mould clay with a closed fist."

Then he set the stone down gently.

"And most of all, Apeksha, it's about *permission*—not from the world, but from yourself. Are you willing to believe that your dreams matter? Are you willing to trust that the universe is not testing you, but waiting for you to take your place in the co-creation of your life?"

He leaned closer, his voice now a quiet ember.

"You must bury the belief that you are helpless. Burn the script that says, 'Who am I to try?' Shatter the ceiling of 'Maybe someday' and replace it with, 'Why not now?'"

The morning breeze grew stronger for a moment, rustling through the banyan leaves like applause from the invisible.

Guruji closed his eyes and said, "When you finally choose to become the sculptor of your own story, life does not resist you. It partners with you. It sends you signs, allies, moments of grace. But it all begins with one brave act: surrendering who you were told to be, to become who you truly are."

The circle remained silent, but in that silence was the sound of inner walls beginning to crumble, of unseen doors slowly creaking open.

Apeksha lowered her gaze, not out of doubt, but out of reverence. In her chest, something old had shifted—an ache, an armour, a forgotten truth.

Guruji smiled, sensing her awakening.

"To move from dreamer to creator," he said, "is not to control life—but to collaborate with it. It is not to demand outcomes—but to align your inner world so clearly, that the outer world has no choice but to echo it."

Guruji, after a long, contemplative silence that felt like an unspoken blessing, opened his eyes slowly. The quiet around him seemed to lean in, listening to his very breath.

He looked at each of them with that serene intensity, then said softly,

"Let us gather in Shambav Hall after an hour."

With a nod that carried both invitation and instruction, he slowly rose from his asana, his palms folding in a gentle Atma Namaste, before walking away with the same grace that had followed him since dawn.

The group gently began to disperse, their silence not empty, but full—full of the echoes of insight, the stirrings of questions, and the deep inner churn of awakening.

Some wandered barefoot along the garden paths, brushing their fingers across the dew-kissed petals of hibiscus and jasmine. Others stood still under trees, eyes closed, allowing the wind to cleanse what no words could.

Akshaya, Vasudeva, and a few others made their way toward the refreshment centre, where the aroma of freshly brewed coffee and roasted lentils wrapped the space like a warm shawl. They found a quiet table beneath a thatched canopy, cups in hand, steam curling into the cool morning air.

Akshaya took a sip, smiled, and leaned back. "Do you remember the story Guruji once told us," he began, "about the young musician who could never hear his own music?"

Vasudeva tilted his head. "No… I don't think I've heard that one."

Akshaya's eyes twinkled.

"There was once a gifted young sitar player named Ahaan, who lived in a coastal town not far from here. He had magic in his fingers, and yet… he was always filled with doubt. Every time he played, he'd glance nervously at the crowd, seeking approval. If they smiled, he smiled. If they frowned, his music faltered."

He paused to sip his coffee, letting the warmth flow with the memory.

"One day, an old man came to him after a performance. He said, 'Your sitar sings, but you don't. You play *through* fear, not *from* your soul.'

'How do I fix that?' Ahaan asked.

The old man replied, 'Go to the hills. Find the echo cave. Play there every morning until you stop needing an answer back.'"

Vasudeva leaned in. "What happened?"

Akshaya smiled, eyes soft.

"He went. For days, the cave only gave him back his own hesitations. But slowly, as the silence of the cave refused to reward or punish him, something shifted. He began playing not for applause, but for the sheer beauty of sound itself. The cave became his companion, not his critic."

There was a silence at the table now—not awkward, but reverent.

"When he returned to the town," Akshaya said, "people wept when he played. Not because he was technically better, but because he was free. His music had become a prayer."

Vasudeva looked down at his cup. "That's what this morning felt like, under the banyan tree. Like we were being asked to stop performing for life—and just live."

Akshaya nodded.

"Exactly. That's what Guruji meant. Manifestation doesn't happen through forced effort… but through inner harmony. Through surrender to the silence that no longer demands to be filled."

At the next table, Padma, Nita, and a few others had overheard the story. Something in their eyes glistened—not with tears, but with that gentle ache that comes when truth knocks softly on the door of the heart.

Padma rose, adjusting her shawl. **"Shall we?"** she said.

Nita smiled, her voice barely above a whisper.

**"Yes… it's time."**

And together, as if drawn by an invisible thread, they began their walk toward **Shambav Hall**, the pathway lined with marigolds and prayer flags dancing in the breeze. The air held a golden stillness, the kind that only exists between realisation and transformation.

Inside their hearts, the story of Ahaan played softly—a quiet reminder that the soul always knows the way back to its own music… if only we stop long enough to listen.

# PART ONE

## The Foundations of Manifestation

*"Manifestation is not magic—it is the silent architecture of belief, emotion, and unwavering intent constructing your future, moment by moment."*

- *Shree Shambav*

# CHAPTER I
## The Invisible Sculptor of Reality

*"The universe is not responding to your words, but to the vibration behind them—your true intentions."*

- Shree Shambav

### Synopsis:

*Manifestation is not a fleeting trend or a fashionable self-help idea—it is a timeless, universal principle embedded within the very essence of existence. This work invites readers to gently dismantle their inherited beliefs about life, success, and happiness, and open themselves to a deeper truth: that thoughts, emotions, intentions, and actions are not isolated fragments, but living forces that continuously shape the fabric of our reality.*

*Every human being is already manifesting their world—not occasionally, but in every moment, whether they are conscious of it or not. The message unfolds with the realisation that manifestation is not a matter of wishful thinking; it is a sacred dance between personal consciousness and the intelligent universe, a co-creative process that begins the moment one becomes aware of it.*

*With poetic insight and practical depth, this journey leads the reader from passivity to purpose—from being a silent observer of life to becoming a deliberate architect of destiny. It offers an awakening into the unseen, subtle forces that sculpt not only what we experience, but who we become.*

As the serene air settled within the sacred expanse of Shambav Hall, it felt as though time itself had taken a reverent breath—pausing to honour the quiet majesty of the moment. The stillness was not empty; it was brimming with presence. It pulsed gently, as though the very walls—etched with the memory of ancient chants and silent meditations—were holding space like silent sentinels of grace. Each corner of the hall whispered of countless seekers who had once wept, wondered, and awakened within its embrace.

Beyond the latticed windows, golden sunlight spilled through like liquid prayer, casting shifting patterns upon the floor—soft mosaics that danced with the wind, as if invisible hands were sketching blessings across the ground. The simplicity of the space did not diminish its depth; it amplified it. The hall was bare of ornament, yet rich with the sacred—the kind of quiet that does not hush the soul but stirs it.

There was a hum beneath the silence, a sacred vibration that soothed the mind's noise and made space for the heart's remembering. It was as if the hall itself had become a bridge between the seen and the unseen—a threshold where the soul could finally hear its own truth again.

*Roopa asked, "Guruji, what is the difference between passive wishing and intentional manifestation, and how does understanding this shift our role from a hopeful dreamer to an active creator of our life?"*

Guruji's eyes shimmered with a stillness that came not from the absence of thought, but from the fullness of wisdom. He gazed at Roopa for a long moment, not in silence, but in the kind of pause that allows truth to bloom in the heart before it's spoken.

He finally said, his voice soft yet carrying the weight of mountains, "Roopa… there is a vast river that flows between wishing and manifesting. Many stand on its banks, tossing their dreams like petals into the current, hoping the river will carry them somewhere meaningful. But manifestation is not about waiting for the river to deliver you—it is about becoming the river itself."

The room grew even quieter. A few birds chirped beyond the hall, as if echoing his words.

He continued, "Wishing is passive—it arises from longing without responsibility. It leans heavily on hope, often laced with fear or doubt. It says, *'I want this… but I don't know if I'm worthy of it, capable of it, or even meant to have it.'* But manifestation… true, intentional manifestation… is the sacred act of declaring your worth, your clarity, your alignment with the life you are ready to live."

Guruji's hand reached down to the earth beside his asana, where a simple seed had been placed earlier by a devotee— perhaps unconsciously, perhaps divinely guided.

He lifted it gently and said, "This seed… does not wish to become a tree. It does not sit in the soil hoping someone will turn it into something greater. No. It *knows*. It holds within it the blueprint of roots, bark, leaves, shade, and fruit. It requires nourishment, yes. It requires sunlight and rain. But it's becoming inevitable—*because it is not doubting its truth.*"

Roopa's eyes welled up, not with sorrow, but with the deep recognition of something ancient stirring in her soul.

Guruji's gaze softened further. "When you manifest, you are not begging the universe. You are partnering with it. You are saying, 'This is the reality I choose to align with, not just with my words, but with my thoughts, my actions, my emotions, and my energy.' It is not about forcing. It is not about control. It is about coherence. About stepping into the frequency of the life that already exists on a higher octave of your current awareness."

He looked around at everyone in Shambav Hall, now entranced in contemplative silence.

"To wish is to speak to the sky. To manifest is to listen to the earth—and become the bridge between both."

The golden light now fully bathed the hall in warmth, as if nature itself was bowing to the truth spoken in its midst.

And in that moment, something subtle shifted within each heart present. A quiet understanding settled: that creation was not a gift reserved for the few, but a birthright dormant in them all—waiting only for intention to awaken it.

The hall held its breath as Akshaya's voice rose gently above the stillness.

*"Guruji,"* he asked, his tone both reverent and vulnerable, *"how do belief systems, whether conscious or unconscious, silently dictate the limits of what we allow ourselves to manifest in our daily reality?"*

Guruji's eyes softened with a timeless knowing, as if he had been waiting for this question to emerge from the sacred stillness of the hall.

He closed his eyes briefly, drawing in a breath that felt older than the walls themselves.

"Akshaya," he began, "belief is like the soil in which the seeds of your life are sown. The quality of that soil—whether it's fertile with possibility or hardened with doubt—determines what will grow."

The room listened, still and silent.

"Let me tell you a story."

Many years ago, in a quiet village not far from here, there was a boy named Arvind who loved the sky. Every day, he would stare up at the clouds and imagine building a machine that could help people fly. He sketched, he dreamed, he experimented—but every time he shared his vision, the elders would laugh and say, 'Such things are for the gods, not for boys born to till the land.'

Over time, the laughter grew louder than his dreams, and though his heart still lifted every time he saw a bird in flight, he packed away his drawings, believing the sky was not meant for him.

Years passed. One day, a group of engineers visited the village to build a wind turbine. Arvind, now older and quieter, watched them work. One of the engineers, noticing his curiosity, invited him to help. Within days, Arvind's natural talent began to shine. The engineer asked, 'Why didn't you ever study this?' Arvind only smiled, his eyes clouded. 'Because I believed I couldn't.'"

Guruji paused, letting the silence deepen the lesson.

"And that," he said gently, "is how belief works. Not with thunder or lightning, but like a whisper in the dark—just loud enough to keep you small."

He looked into Akshaya's eyes, and then at everyone in the room.

*"Most people do not manifest what they want because they are unknowingly loyal to what they believe they deserve. These beliefs are not always born from logic—they are inherited, absorbed, reinforced, often rooted in past wounds, cultural conditioning, or unexamined fear."*

He continued:

"Imagine your mind as a vast mansion, yet you live in only one dimly lit room because someone once told you the rest of the house was haunted. Manifestation begins when you gather the courage to walk through the locked doors and say, 'This is mine to live in. This is mine to light.'"

A hush fell over the hall—heavy, not with silence, but with presence. A few eyes shimmered with tears. Others sat with their hands clasped over their hearts, as if some invisible weight had just been lifted.

Guruji leaned back, his voice now a whisper.

"If you wish to manifest consciously, do not begin by asking 'What do I want?' Instead, ask, 'What do I believe I am allowed to receive?' That answer… will change your life."

The golden hush inside Shambav Hall seemed to deepen as Padma rose gently from her seat, her hands loosely clasped in front of her heart.

*"Guruji," she asked softly, "in what ways do emotions serve as the 'fuel' of manifestation—and how can unexamined emotional patterns either accelerate or sabotage the creation of our desired experiences?"*

Guruji looked at her with eyes that held oceans—of memory, compassion, and understanding. He nodded slowly, as though her question had not only pierced the air, but also touched the soul of the moment itself.

"Padma," he began, his voice a blend of warmth and reverence, "emotion is not merely a reaction—it is a vibration, a frequency that flows directly into the field of creation. It is the current that carries your intention across the invisible bridge between thought and reality."

He paused, then added:

"Think of manifestation as a bow and arrow. Your desire is the arrow. Your belief is the direction. But emotion… emotion is the strength of the draw. Without it, your arrow barely leaves the bowstring. With it, it can soar across time and space."

The room fell into a deeper silence.

"But," Guruji continued, "if your emotional energy is tangled in fear, resentment, guilt, or old grief that you haven't yet seen or healed—it's like pouring muddy water into the engine of your dreams. It clogs, it delays, it redirects, often without you realising it."

He leaned forward now, his hands gently folded in his lap.

Guruji said, "Let me tell you a story."

Years ago, there was a woman named Charumathi who had a beautiful voice. From the time she was a child, people said her singing felt like prayer in motion. She dreamed of sharing her music with the world. She recorded demos, sent them to studios, and prayed with all her heart.

But every opportunity seemed to slip away. Either something would go wrong, or people would simply stop responding. One day, she came to me, her voice trembling with frustration. 'Why is the universe ignoring my heart's deepest longing?' she asked.

I looked into her eyes and said, 'What do you feel when you sing?' She paused and whispered, 'I feel unworthy… as though someone is going to tell me I'm not enough.'

And there it was. Her song was beautiful, but it was wrapped in the vibration of self-doubt. The universe wasn't ignoring her—it was echoing her own hidden emotion.

Guruji turned to Padma, his gaze steady and filled with compassion.

"This is how emotions serve as both messengers and magnifiers. Whatever you feel—deeply, consistently, truthfully—adds velocity to your intentions. But if your heart is weighed down by unseen wounds, those emotions become shadows, quietly pulling your reality in directions you don't consciously choose."

Guruji looked around the hall.

"We are not punished by our emotions—we are guided by them. They do not betray us; they reveal what has been buried. If you want to manifest a higher reality, you must first become intimate with your inner weather. You must ask: What am I truly feeling beneath the surface of my desires?"

A tear rolled down Padma's cheek—not from sadness, but from resonance, from something ancient being remembered.

"Emotions," Guruji said, "are the language the soul speaks before the mind begins to explain. Listen to them. Heal them. And they will become the wind beneath the wings of your becoming."

Vasudeva, who often listened more than he spoke, his eyes held the weight of reflection, but also the lightness of one who seeks not just answers, but understanding.

*"Guruji,"* he began, *his voice calm and steady, "If thoughts are the blueprint and emotions are the energy, where does focused intention fit into the process of turning our inner vision into external reality?"*

A hush followed, not from uncertainty, but from the sacred space that opens when a question touches the very marrow of inquiry.

Guruji's face lit with a quiet smile, as if Vasudeva's words were a key that had just unlocked a door waiting to be opened.

"Ah, Vasudeva," he said, his voice resonant and serene, "what a beautiful bridge you build between mind and heart. Your question holds the architecture of the entire manifestation process."

He folded his palms softly, as if to contain the essence of what he was about to share.

"Imagine you are an architect designing a temple," Guruji began. "Your thoughts draft the blueprint—what it should look like, how it should feel. Your emotions pour in the energy—whether it is a temple of hope, joy, doubt, or fear. But intention… intention is the hand that picks up the chisel. It's the sacred will that begins the work of sculpting the invisible into form."

He paused, allowing the metaphor to settle.

"Without focused intention," he continued, "your thoughts remain as sketches in the clouds, and your emotions, however powerful, remain like rivers without direction. But when intention is harnessed—clear, committed, and anchored—it becomes the alignment point between the inner and the outer worlds."

Then he leaned back slightly, his eyes gleaming with memory.

Guruji said, "Let me tell you a story."

There was once a potter named Bhargav who lived at the edge of a desert village. For years, he dreamed of creating a unique kind of vessel—one that would keep water cool in the harshest sun, and be beautiful enough to offer in temples. He would often speak of it to his friends, sketch its shape, imagine its texture.

His emotions ran deep. He cried when he failed. He laughed in delight when a small piece came out right. He prayed, visualised, and felt it all. But for years, the perfect vessel never came.

One day, a wandering sadhu passed through the village and asked Bhargav, "Why do you only dream of the vessel? Why not decide to make it?"

Bhargav was stunned. "But I have decided," he replied.

The sadhu smiled. "No," he said gently. "You have desired it. You have even felt it. But you have not yet committed to it as your sacred task. Focused intention is not a passing breeze—it is the unwavering flame. Until you light that flame and guard it with your life, your dreams will hover just beyond the horizon."

Guruji looked around the hall, where each listener sat motionless, the story echoing within their own unfinished dreams.

"Focused intention," he said softly, "is the vow the soul makes to creation. It is the moment when you stop negotiating with your fears and start honouring your purpose. It turns your desire into direction, your energy into embodiment."

He closed his eyes briefly, then added:

"The universe responds not just to your longing, but to your loyalty to that longing."

Vasudeva nodded, slowly, something within him shifting—not as a thought, but as a quiet clarity, a subtle resolve. He had understood—not just the words, but the call.

"Let each of us," Guruji concluded, "become not just dreamers, but architects. Not just feelers, but sculptors. With thought as vision, emotion as power, and intention as sacred action, there is nothing we cannot shape."

# CHAPTER II
## The Language of the Universe

*"The universe does not speak in words—it hums in frequencies. To understand its language, one must first learn to listen, not with ears, but with awareness."*

– Shree Shambav

### Synopsis

*This invitation calls the reader to release the old lens through which reality appears fixed and unchangeable, and instead awaken to a deeper truth: everything is energy—including who we are. Thoughts, emotions, intentions, and even the tangible objects around us are simply expressions of vibration at different frequencies. When we come to understand this fundamental nature of existence, we begin to unlock the ability to align with the rhythm of the universe itself. It is in this alignment that conscious creation becomes possible. Suddenly, manifestation is no longer a distant concept, but a living dialogue between your inner world and the energetic field of the cosmos—a dance of awareness where every feeling and focus is a step toward shaping the life you were meant to live.*

The sacred stillness in Shambav Hall had matured into a quiet attentiveness—a presence that one could feel rather than describe. Outside, a gentle breeze rustled the leaves of the ancient banyan tree, and the soft cadence of nature seemed to harmonise with the rhythms within. The hall was not merely a space—it had become a vessel for transformation, a listening womb where hearts opened like petals to truth.

Vidyarthi, whose name itself meant "the seeker of knowledge," sat forward. His gaze was steady, but beneath it was a deep yearning—not just to understand, but to embody. He folded his hands and asked:

*"Guruji, if everything in the universe is energy vibrating at different frequencies, how do our thoughts and emotions influence the energetic environment we live in?"*

Guruji's eyes lit up—not with amusement, but with reverence. He had always loved it when someone touched the subtle realms with such honesty.

He closed his eyes briefly, then opened them slowly, as if retrieving something from the vast, unseen.

"Vidyarthi," he began, "you've just stepped into the sacred science of the soul."

The hall leaned in.

"Everything, every star, every breath, every unspoken word—is energy," Guruji said. "Energy is not just movement; it is intelligence. It responds. It listens. It harmonises. And your thoughts and emotions? They are the tuning forks of your inner instrument. They determine the song you send out to the cosmos."

He looked around, then continued.

"Imagine a lake at dawn. Still. Clear. Now throw a pebble—a thought—into its surface. Instantly, ripples spread out. Add emotion to it, and it's like adding colour and intensity to that ripple. Fear makes the ripple chaotic. Love makes it expansive. Joy adds a melody. Anger makes it crash."

Guruji stood and slowly walked toward the open window. The light caressed his robes, as though the universe itself bowed to what was about to be shared.

Guruji said, "Let me tell you a story."

In a remote Himalayan village, there was a woman named Maithili. She was known not for her wealth or wisdom, but for the way her presence changed the air around her. When she entered a room, people stopped arguing. When she sat with the sick, they felt lighter. No one could explain it, but all could feel it.

One day, a young sceptic from the city came to stay in the village. He watched Maithili closely. She spoke little, worked humbly, and never gave advice. But he noticed something: every morning, she would rise before the sun, sit by the river, and whisper things—not to anyone, but to the wind.

One morning, he followed her. "What are you saying?" he finally asked.

She smiled and replied, "I am tuning my heart."

"Tuning?" he asked.

She nodded. "My thoughts are like strings. If they are slack, I feel heavy. If they are tight, I feel restless. But if they are tuned with love and presence, I become a song the world can hear, even in silence."

The sceptic said nothing. But that evening, when Maithili entered the room, he too felt it—the air changed.

Guruji turned back toward the hall, his voice now a whisper carried by silence.

"We are not separate from the energetic ocean we live in. Our thoughts shape its waves. Our emotions colour its light. Every fear contracts the space around us. Every love expands it. And when we master the tuning of this inner instrument, we don't just change our life—we subtly re-tune the whole universe around us."

He paused.

"The universe is not waiting for you to be perfect. It is waiting for you to become aware. Because once you do, even a single intentional thought, aligned with emotion, can ripple across creation."

Vidyarthi sat motionless. He wasn't just hearing—he was absorbing. In that moment, he wasn't just a seeker. He was a song waiting to be sung, a ripple just beginning to move.

*Aastha lifted her gaze toward Guruji and asked, with a voice clear yet tender, "Guruji, how does the vibrational alignment between your desires and your current emotional state affect the speed and clarity of manifestation?"*

Guruji closed his eyes, as if entering a deeper current beneath the surface of thought. A peaceful smile emerged—one that carried the memory of oceans and lifetimes.

"Aastha," he said gently, "Desire is not the enemy of peace. It is the invitation. But it is not desire alone that creates. It is the frequency with which it is carried."

He paused, letting the words settle.

"You see, every desire emits a signal—like a lighthouse beam. But if your emotional state sends out a contradictory signal—of doubt, fear, or unworthiness—then your inner vibration becomes like a storm-tossed sea, scattering the beam. The universe cannot respond clearly to confusion. It mirrors coherence."

Guruji motioned with his hand, drawing an invisible wave in the air.

"Imagine two musical instruments—one finely tuned, the other not. If you try to play a melody between them, the sound will be dissonant, jarring. But if both are in tune, even a single note resonates like truth. Manifestation is like this. Your desire is one instrument, your emotional state is the other. When they are aligned, the universe hears the harmony and responds swiftly."

He turned slightly and looked out toward the old mango tree visible through the window.

Guruji said, "Let me share a story."

There was once a potter named Raghava in a quiet village much like this one. Every day, he would shape clay pots and whisper his dreams into them—dreams of travelling, of singing before great crowds, of seeing the ocean.

But year after year, he remained in the same village, shaping the same pots, whispering the same dreams. One day, a wandering monk arrived and noticed the fire in Raghava's eyes and the heaviness in his heart.

"What keeps you here?" the monk asked.

Raghava smiled sadly. "My dreams are too big. My life is too small."

The monk sat beside him and said, "It is not your dreams that are too big. It is your belief that is too small."

He handed Raghava a bowl of water and said, "Now sing your dream into this bowl." Raghava did, softly. The monk then dropped a stone into it. The ripples grew wide, but then faded.

"This is how your desires behave when your emotions do not believe in them," the monk said. "They ripple, but then they vanish. Now… try again—but this time, feel it in your bones. Feel it like it's already true."

Raghava hesitated, then closed his eyes. He sang again—but this time, with tears of certainty. The monk smiled. "Now, the ripples will reach the ocean."

Guruji turned back toward Aastha, his voice soft yet powerful.

"Your emotional state is the soil into which your desire is planted. If it is rich with trust, joy, and presence, your desire grows swiftly—like a seed knowing it is welcome. But if the soil is dry with fear or doubt, even the strongest seed may struggle to sprout."

He continued,

"So ask not just what you want from the universe. Ask what energy you are broadcasting while you wait. Is it fear disguised as hope? Or is it trust dressed in surrender?"

The room held its breath. And in that stillness, many recognised their own patterns—the times they wanted deeply but feared quietly, the times they wished loudly but doubted silently.

Aastha bowed slightly, her heart moved, not by information—but by remembrance.

She now knew: manifestation is not just about wanting. It is about becoming the frequency of what you seek.

The light filtering into Shambav Hall now felt warmer, more intimate—like the golden embrace of truth drawing ever closer.

Abhirami, whose name carried the essence of the divine feminine, her voice, when it emerged, was steady and sincere, touched by the longing for a deeper understanding:

*"Guruji, in what ways can shifting your perception from matter-based thinking to energy-based awareness transform your relationships, choices, and life path?"*

Guruji looked at her, eyes soft with knowing. He waited for a few breaths—as if to honour the sacredness of the question itself—before responding.

"Abhirami," he began, "when we live in a matter-based reality, we see the world as fixed—objects, people, outcomes, roles. Everything appears separate and solid. But when we shift into energy-based awareness, the veil lifts. We begin to sense that nothing is static. Everything is in motion, vibrating, exchanging, evolving."

"Matter-based thinking focuses on the surface—what you see, touch, and name. But energy-based awareness feels what is unseen, senses what is becoming. One sees the mask, the other feels the soul behind it."

He turned his gaze to the group and continued with an analogy.

"Think of life like a vast ocean," he said. "Matter-based thinking is like watching the surface—waves, ripples, foam. It reacts to storms and fears the unknown. But energy-based awareness is like diving below, into the deep stillness beneath the turbulence. Down there, everything is connected. Everything responds not to control—but to presence."

Guruji said, "Let me narrate a story: Long ago, in a small Himalayan village, there lived a healer named Devayani. People came from far and wide—not because she gave them herbs, but because of how they felt in her presence. She never spoke of illness. She spoke of imbalance. She didn't ask, 'What hurts?' but 'What shifted within you that stopped flowing?'"

"One day, a troubled woman came to her, heartbroken and bitter after years of betrayal. Devayani offered her no sympathy—only a mirror and a bowl of still water."

'Look into the mirror,' she said. 'Tell me what you see.'

The woman replied, 'I see a tired, broken woman who has been hurt too many times.'

Then Devayani gestured to the bowl. 'Now, place your hand in the water and stir it.'

The woman did, and the reflection vanished into chaos. Devayani smiled. 'This is what your energy looks like when your emotions are unacknowledged. You try to fix the reflection, but the water is still agitated. Sit beside it. Breathe. Don't touch it. Just feel.'

Slowly, the water calmed. The woman looked again, and the image returned—clear, gentle, unbroken. In that moment, she realised: her healing would not come from changing the world, but from attuning her energy to peace."

Guruji looked back at Abhirami.

"When you shift from matter to energy," he said softly, "you no longer ask, 'What can I get from this person, this job, this situation?' Instead, you ask, 'What am I radiating into this relationship? What frequency am I contributing?'"

"You stop chasing outcomes. You start calibrating presence. This transforms everything—because now, you are not reacting to life, you are relating with it."

His voice slowed as he concluded:

"Your life path begins to unfold not by force or fear, but by resonance. What belongs to you comes—not because you grab it, but because you align with it. And in that state, you do not walk a path—you become the path."

The silence that followed wasn't empty. It was rich. Potent. Charged with the collective recognition of a truth they all remembered but had rarely lived.

Abhirami's eyes shimmered—not from sadness, but from that rare feeling when something you've always felt finally has words.

And as she bowed her head in gratitude, it became clear—this wasn't just a question answered.

It was a life reoriented.

Kiran gave a thoughtful look on his face. His question carried the tone of quiet urgency—the kind born not from doubt, but from sincere yearning.

*"Guruji,"* he began softly, *"how can daily practices like meditation, mindful breathing, and intentional thinking raise your personal energetic frequency to align with the life you seek to manifest?"*

Guruji's eyes gleamed, as if Kiran had touched a thread that led directly into the heart of sacred remembrance.

"Kiran," Guruji said with warmth, "imagine your life is a radio. The station you receive depends not on what's being broadcast—but on what frequency you're tuned to. Joy, love, peace—they are always present, just as certain stations are always transmitting. But unless you tune yourself correctly, all you'll hear is static."

He paused, letting the metaphor settle like morning mist.

"Daily practices," he continued, "are how we tune ourselves. They are not rituals for perfection. They are invitations to presence."

He leaned forward slightly and added, "Let me share with you a story."

"There was once a man named Dhanan, a gifted potter who lived at the edge of a quiet forest. Each morning, before touching a single lump of clay, he would walk barefoot into the forest and sit beside a silent stream. He would listen—not to words, but to the rhythm of breath, the song of birds, the murmur of water.

One day, a traveller came and asked, 'Why do you waste time here when you could make more pots, earn more money, gain more recognition?'

Dhanan smiled and said, 'Before my hands shape the clay, I must first shape the stillness within me. The pot I create reflects the silence I carry. Without it, I would only produce noise in form.'

And so, his pots became famous—not for their beauty alone, but for the peace people felt when holding them. They carried his inner frequency."

Guruji looked at Kiran with softness.

"Meditation," he said, "is how you return to your original frequency. Mindful breathing is how you cleanse the interference. Intentional thinking is how you plant the seeds of your inner garden."

He gestured toward the group.

"You don't attract what you want. You attract what you are. And what you are is what you practice daily—not in grand gestures, but in the quiet ways you greet your breath, your thoughts, your emotions."

"When you sit in stillness each morning, you are not doing nothing. You are resetting your compass. You are clearing the fog. You are whispering to the universe, 'I am ready.' And the universe, like a mirror, responds not with judgment, but with reflection."

Kiran nodded slowly, his breath deepening, as if something inside him had gently shifted.

Guruji continued:

"The greatest transformations begin not in moments of greatness, but in the small, sacred choices we make each day—whether we breathe with awareness or rush unconsciously; whether we judge ourselves or hold space for our becoming."

A hush fell over the group—a hush that wasn't empty, but full. Full of inner commitment. Full of readiness. Full of the silent promise: I will show up for my own becoming.

And in that moment, without moving an inch, every soul in the hall took one step closer to the life they were born to manifest.

Guruji, after a long pause, asked all the devotees to take a break for the day's meal. After having the midday meal, some rested under large trees, some went for a stroll, and some settled back in Shambav Hall. Padma, Akshaya and the others settled under a large banyan tree…

## A Story of Stillness and Seeing

The grand banyan tree stood like a sacred witness, its colossal roots emerging from the earth like the arms of an ancient sage in meditation. The shade it cast was cool, the sunlight filtered through its layered canopy, dappling the ground in shifting patterns—almost like fragments of truth revealing themselves to those who dared to pause.

Padma lay back against the base of the tree, tracing circles in the dust with her fingers. Akshaya sat nearby, his eyes half-closed, cradling a cup of warm herbal tea. Sofia, Bhavya, Aarna, and Dev all gathered in the hush of that moment, drawn together by something more than curiosity—it was the quiet pull of shared wonder.

Alice turned toward Apeksha, smiling.

"You mentioned a story this morning… something Guruji did that stayed with you?"

Apeksha's face softened with the warmth of memory. "Yes," she said, "a moment that taught me more than any book, lecture, or theory ever could."

"It was a retreat just like this—summer, intense, and emotionally raw. We were a smaller group back then. One morning, a man named Anay, a deeply rational and sceptical seeker, stood up during a session with a voice full of agitation.

He said, 'Guruji, I respect you, but all this talk about energy, surrender, manifestation—it feels too abstract. Isn't action what really matters? Isn't this just a poetic distraction from real-world work?'

He wasn't rude. He was honest. But the room held its breath. Everyone looked to Guruji for an answer. He didn't speak immediately. He just... smiled, that mysterious smile that somehow held galaxies in it.

Then, very calmly, Guruji got up and walked out of the hall without a word. Confused, we all followed him. He led us through the winding trails, past the mango orchard, to a small hill where an old water wheel stood still under the midday sun.

The wheel hadn't moved in years. Dust had settled in its grooves, weeds growing around its base. Guruji asked Anay, 'Can this wheel turn?'

Anay nodded, 'Yes, with water.'

Guruji said, 'So the structure is not the problem?'

'No,' Anay said.

Guruji then pointed to the dry canal nearby. 'That's your mind,' he said gently. 'And the water that fuels the wheel—that's your awareness and alignment. Without flow, even the most intricate structure stays still.'

He paused, then added, 'You speak of action, and that is good. But action without alignment is effort without effect. You may build great things, but if your inner stream is dry, there's no life to move them.'

'We don't meditate or manifest to avoid work,' he said, 'We do so to ensure our work flows from clarity, not compulsion. From presence, not pressure.'

Apeksha looked around the group now, her voice softer.

"It wasn't a lecture that changed Anay. It was that moment under the sun, beside a forgotten wheel. Guruji didn't convince him with logic—he helped him see. That's the difference. That's his gift."

Sofia whispered, "It's almost as if he speaks to a part of us we forget exists…"

Bhavya added, "We think transformation happens in big moments, but sometimes it's just… a walk, a wheel, a sentence."

Dev leaned forward, thoughtful.

"And the mind is that canal, isn't it? So many of us are trying to turn our lives' wheels dry. No wonder we feel stuck."

Akshaya looked up toward the thick banyan leaves above them.

"Stillness is not absence. It's preparation. It's the gathering of the waters before the flow."

The group sat in silence, not because they had nothing to say, but because they had suddenly too much to feel. Under that tree, amidst the roots of the earth and the roots of their own becoming, something shifted quietly within them.

The banyan, ever silent, ever still, swayed gently in the afternoon breeze—as if it too had once heard this story, and never forgotten it.

And slowly, they rose—not hurriedly, but with the grace of those who had seen something worth carrying within. As they made their way toward Shambav Hall, it wasn't just their feet that moved forward—it was their presence, their perception, and perhaps, their purpose.

# CHAPTER III

## The Divine Dialogue

*"As we shift the mirror of our consciousness, the universe reflects the truth of our thoughts, revealing the boundless possibilities of creation."*

– Shree Shambav

### Synopsis

*This exploration takes us deep into the sacred relationship between personal consciousness and the universal intelligence that breathes life into all things. It invites us to see our thoughts, feelings, and actions not as isolated flickers in the dark, but as threads woven into a vast, living tapestry of existence. Our minds are not separate from the cosmos—they are expressions of it. When we begin to align our inner awareness with the intelligence that moves the stars, creation flows not through effort, but through harmony. We are not asking the universe for favours; we are co-creating with it. Manifestation, then, becomes a natural communion—a divine dialogue where our intentions ripple through the unseen, and the universe responds with grace and precision.*

After a brief pause, as silence gently settled like sacred mist within the stillness of Shambav Hall...

Sam leaned forward slightly and asked, his voice sincere yet searching, *"Guruji, how does personal consciousness interact with the greater universal intelligence to shape the reality we experience?"*

Guruji closed his eyes for a moment. Then, with a voice both gentle and grounded, he said, "Sam, imagine standing on the shore of a vast ocean at dawn. The ocean before you is the universal intelligence—boundless, deep, and aware of ways the mind can hardly fathom. And you, the individual, are like a flute lying quietly in the sand. Alone, the flute makes no sound. But when the breeze—your consciousness—moves through it with intent and presence, music is born. That music is your reality."

He let the words linger in the stillness before continuing.

"You see, personal consciousness is not a separate drop from the ocean; it is a wave formed by the ocean's own will. And yet, within each wave is the potential to rise, to choose direction, and to shape the shore it touches. The universe is not watching us from afar; it is participating through us. Your thoughts, feelings, and choices are not whispers in the dark—they are signals sent into the vast field of intelligence that surrounds and fills us. When these signals are chaotic, reality becomes fragmented. But when they are aligned—rooted in clarity, love, and purpose—reality responds with astonishing precision."

Guruji's eyes gently scanned the gathering, and he spoke with a softness that stirred something ancient in their hearts.

"Let me tell you a story," he said.

"There was once a young woman named Anaya who lived in a small, coastal village. She believed life was something that simply happened to her—waves of fate, storms of chance. One year, a terrible drought dried up their wells. Crops withered. People grew restless. Most villagers resigned themselves to the suffering, believing the gods were punishing them. But Anaya… she did something unusual. Every morning, she walked to the edge of the dried riverbed and sang. She sang songs of rain, of abundance, of water returning to kiss the earth. People laughed at her, called her foolish.

But she kept singing.

One elder, moved by her unwavering devotion, asked her, 'Why do you sing to a river that has abandoned us?'

She replied, 'The river has not left us. We stopped believing we were its voice. I sing not just to remember the rain—I sing to call it back.'

And one morning, as her song rose to the sky, the clouds gathered—first faintly, then with purpose. Rain came. Not a miracle, but a reunion."

Guruji paused. "Anaya wasn't just wishing. She was aligning. Her personal consciousness—her belief, her emotion, her song—was in harmony with the greater field of intelligence. The universe did not simply grant her a favour. It responded to her as an echo responds to a call."

He leaned forward slightly, his voice a near whisper.

"Reality is not solid stone—it is soft clay in the hands of consciousness. Shape it not through force, but through awareness. Through song. Through presence."

Alice, her voice tinged with both wonder and seeking, turned to Guruji and asked:

*"Guruji, what does it mean for consciousness to be 'in alignment' with the universal intelligence, and how can we achieve this state?"*

Guruji gently opened his eyes, as if returning from the quiet sanctuary of the cosmos within. His gaze, soft yet piercing, settled on Alice for a moment. Then, with a voice that carried both silence and sound, he began.

"To be in alignment," he said, "is not to become something new, but to remember who you are beneath all the layers of noise, fear, conditioning, and desire."

He reached down and picked up a dry leaf. Holding it up, he continued:

"Imagine this leaf," he said, turning it in his palm, "once part of the tree, once green and vibrant, drawing life directly from the roots. It did not strive or force its way into being—it simply received what was already flowing through the tree. That is alignment. It is not controlled. It is a connection."

The group listened, the leaf rustling faintly in his fingers like a whisper from nature itself.

"Alignment with universal intelligence," he continued, "is like sailing with the wind instead of against it. Your consciousness is the sail. The universe is the wind. If your sail is raised with clarity, trust, and openness, you move with grace. If it is torn by doubt, or furled tight with resistance, the wind cannot guide you, no matter how strong it blows."

He paused, letting the analogy sink in. Then Guruji told a story.

"Years ago," Guruji said, "there was a young man named Raghav, who came to this very village searching for purpose. He was brilliant, restless, and deeply sceptical. He had read every book on philosophy, tried countless practices, yet he felt lost. One morning, during a walking meditation, I asked him to stop trying. 'Stop trying to find alignment,' I said, 'and start noticing where you've been fighting it.' He laughed—confused—but I left him with that."

"That evening, he returned with tears in his eyes. 'Guruji,' he said, 'all this time, I've been trying to become someone worthy of the universe's help. I never realised I was already a part of it.'"

"That," Guruji said, gently setting the leaf down, "is the key to alignment—not in effort, but in surrender. Not in striving to be perfect, but in trusting that your essence is already divine."

He looked around, his voice like a balm.

"You achieve alignment not by changing who you are, but by removing what you are not—the false beliefs, the fear-based identities, the constant need to control the how and when. Meditation, mindful presence, emotional honesty, and deep trust—these are the practices that polish the mirror of your inner being until it can reflect the light of the universe clearly."

A quiet stillness embraced the circle once more.

After a long, contemplative silence, Sofia's voice rose, clear yet tender, carrying a question that seemed to vibrate with the very yearning of the soul:

*"Guruji, how does the concept of oneness between the personal mind and the universal mind challenge traditional views of individuality and separation?"*

Guruji smiled—a smile not of lips alone, but of being—and for a moment, he simply looked at each face in the room, as if seeing beyond their forms into the timeless essence that lived within each.

Then, in a voice that felt like it was coming from the very heart of the hall itself, he began:

"Sofia," he said, "imagine you are standing before a vast lake at dawn. The surface is so still that the sky—its stars, its clouds, even the first blush of the sun—are reflected perfectly. Now, imagine throwing a pebble into the lake. The ripples move outward, touching every reflection. Was the lake ever separate from the sky? Or was it always one, only disturbed by the smallness of our perception?"

He paused, and the listeners leaned into the silence, feeling the depth of it.

"Individuality," Guruji continued, "is like identifying only with the ripple, forgetting the vastness of the lake beneath it. The personal mind believes itself to be a single wave, struggling against other waves, forgetting it is—and always has been—the entire ocean in motion."

Guruji said, "Let me narrate a story. Years ago, a young woman named Meera came to Shambav Hall. Her life had been shaped by deep sorrow—abandonment, betrayal, isolation. She carried her pain like a second skin. One afternoon, much like this one, she asked me, 'Guruji, if God is everywhere, why do I feel so alone?'"

The hall seemed to hold its breath.

"I gave her a lump of clay and asked her to mould it. She shaped a small cup. I said, 'What is this?' She answered, 'A cup.'

'No,' I said. 'It is clay taking the form of a cup. If you crush it and reshape it, it is still clay. Its essence never changes—only its form.'"

"That day, she realised something profound: she was not her experiences, not her suffering, not her triumphs. She was the substance behind it all—the eternal, formless life that merely takes form for a while."

Guruji's voice deepened, becoming almost a whisper that touched the soul more than the ears:

"The idea of separation is a necessary dream—but it is a dream nonetheless. Behind every name, every face, behind each joy and sorrow, there is only one life moving. When we awaken to this truth, life itself changes—anger softens into understanding, fear dissolves into wonder, and love ceases to be a transaction and becomes our natural state."

The sun's golden rays deepened into a soft amber, washing the hall in a hushed, sacred light.

"To live from this knowing," Guruji said, "is to live as the sky and the ocean—limitless, embracing all, rejecting none."

A profound silence followed—not empty, but full, as if the very stones of Shambav Hall were humming the memory of oneness.

Guruji's voice rose, soft yet echoing through every heart.

*In the stillness between two breaths,*

*I heard the sound of silence speak —*

*not as absence,*

*but as all.*

*Not my name, not my past,*

*not the stories I clutched like broken prayer beads,*

*but something older…*

*a hush that held both stars and sorrow alike.*

*I am not the ripple fearing the storm,*

*but the lake that receives both wind and moonlight.*

*I am not this shape of longing and form —*

*but the formless that takes every form.*

*And when I forgot,*

*Love—not loud,*

*but sure—whispered:*

*'You were never apart.'*

Sofia sat motionless, her hands resting gently on her knees, her heart trembling not from fear, but from a recognition so ancient and deep that it defied words.

It was as if the veil had thinned, and for a brief, shining moment, the wave remembered it was the ocean.

Bhavya, her hands resting lightly in her lap, asked with quiet earnestness, "Guruji, in what ways can we consciously participate in the cosmic dialogue to enhance our manifestations and align our desires with the universal flow?"

Guruji listened without hurry.

He allowed the question to travel fully through the room before he spoke, his voice calm, deliberate, and heavy with understanding.

"Bhavya, most people live as if they are isolated islands—believing that their thoughts, their actions, and their outcomes are entirely separate from the larger fabric of life.

But the truth is different.

Personal consciousness and universal intelligence are not two things. They are like a flame and its warmth—distinguishable only in thought, but inseparable in reality."

He paused, ensuring that the weight of those words anchored deeply.

"When we think of manifestation, we often imagine it as a transaction: 'I want this; I must do something to get it.'

But the deeper view is not transactional—it is relational.

It is a conversation, not a command."

Guruji shifted slightly, leaning into a story that unfolded naturally from within him:

"Years ago, in a village on the other side of the river valley, there lived a farmer named Anay. Anay was hardworking, but he believed that the soil owed him a harvest simply because he planted seeds. Each year, he would till the earth aggressively, sow seeds in a rush, demand rain from the heavens, and grow bitter when nature did not immediately obey.

One particularly dry season, frustrated beyond measure, Anay travelled to an old hermit known to have deep knowledge of the land.

The hermit said to him:

*'You plant your seeds into the soil, but you do not ask the soil if it is ready.*

*You pray for rain, but you do not sit long enough to hear when the clouds are gathering.*

*You see life as an opponent you must conquer, but life is a friend you must learn to listen to.'*

The hermit then guided Anay not just to sow seeds, but to understand the moods of the earth, the seasons of the wind, the silent messages written in the colour of the leaves and the behaviour of the birds.

Over time, Anay stopped farming by force. He began to farm through a relationship.

He learned to prepare the earth when it was willing, not when he demanded. He sowed with patience, harvested with gratitude, and prayed not for rain, but for the wisdom to act in harmony with it.

His fields prospered beyond anything he had ever seen—not because he worked harder, but because he worked with life, not against it."

Guruji's voice deepened further:

"The universe, Bhavya, is not here to be ordered about. It is here to be partnered with.

Consciously participating in the cosmic dialogue means learning to live like Anay—attuned, receptive, responsive.

*Meditation is how we listen.*

*Mindful observation is how we recognise the signs.*

*Emotional clarity is how we speak without confusion.*

*Surrender is how we leave room for the intelligence of life to do what we alone cannot."*

He looked around at the faces gathered under the great dome of Shambav Hall, their eyes reflecting a growing understanding.

"Every desire you hold is an invitation for a conversation with the universe.

If your mind is noisy with fear, urgency, or distrust, you will not hear the answers.

But if you cultivate stillness, if you clear the emotional ground, if you align your energy to trust rather than tension, then the answers will come not as thunder, but as a steady, guiding hand upon your life."

Guruji leaned back, his gaze expansive:

*"Manifestation, in its truest sense, is not about getting everything you want.*

*It is about becoming everything you were meant to be—by entering into a conscious, continuous dialogue with existence itself."*

Bhavya sat still, the words not just touching her intellect but soaking into her very being—as if she had been offered a map back to a home she had forgotten she was already part of.

And within the silent reverence of Shambav Hall, many others felt it too—a soft shift, a realignment, a remembering.

Guruji, after a brief pause and a soft smile, invited all the devotees to take a short break.

The hall slowly exhaled, as if even the stones themselves needed a moment to breathe.

Outside, the evening had draped the landscape in a muted gold. Birds were returning from their long day's work, their wings cutting gentle patterns across the setting sun. The scent of wildflowers floated lazily through the air, mingling with the comforting aroma of fresh herbal tea and brewing coffee.

The place felt sacred, but alive—a meeting ground between the stillness of spirit and the gentle rhythms of life.

Under the great canopy of the Banyan tree, Nita, Lalitha, Rohith, Sujitha, and Espen gathered in a relaxed circle.

Nearby, Padma, Vasudeva, and Akshaya moved about with quiet joy, serving steaming cups of herbal tea and coffee, their laughter carrying lightly on the breeze.

Sujitha cradled her cup with both hands, her eyes thoughtful. After a moment, she said, almost to herself:

"I remember a story my mother always used to tell me when I was little... whenever she pointed to a star."

The group leaned in, curiosity stirring between them.

Sujitha smiled gently, lost in the memory, and began:

"When I was a child, I would often ask my mother what the stars were.

And she would say, 'Each star is a dream, Sujitha—a dream someone dared to dream, but more importantly, a dream someone dared to believe was already alive, long before they could touch it.'

I would look up, confused, because to me, the stars seemed so far away—so unreachable.

One evening, when I was particularly insistent, my mother took me by the hand, and we sat on the porch together under the open sky.

She pointed to a particularly bright star and said, 'That one belongs to a farmer who sowed his fields with hope even when the rains failed him. Another star belongs to a young woman who crossed mountains to build a life where there was none.

And that star over there—the one you think is so distant—is already inside you. It shines because you carry its light, not because you have to reach it.'"

Sujitha paused, her eyes misty with the sweetness of the memory.

"She used to tell me that the dreams and hopes we think are outside of us are not really somewhere else. They live within us, vibrating, waiting for us to recognise them—just like the light of a star that took thousands of years to reach our eyes, yet was always burning."

The group sat quietly, letting the story sink into the marrow of their longings and memories.

It connected deeply with all they had been learning from Guruji—that manifestation is not about *grasping at distant dreams*, but about *recognising the timeless reality* that dreams are already seeded within consciousness itself, awaiting alignment, trust, and nurturing action.

It wasn't about chasing life.

It was about *allowing life* to rise from within.

The wildflowers nearby swayed softly as if nodding in agreement, and the world around them seemed stitched together by an invisible tenderness—the same tenderness that carries seeds through winter, or stars through the endless corridors of time.

After a while, Kiran, who had been watching the deepening sky, sighed contentedly and said, with a touch of reluctance:

"Friends... It's time for the next session."

The group smiled, gathering their cups and folding the story into their hearts like a beloved letter, knowing they would carry it long after the last words of the evening had been spoken.

# CHAPTER IV

## How Entanglement Fuels Manifestation

*"As we observe, we become the creators. Our consciousness doesn't merely witness the world; it shapes it. In the quantum realm, the act of observing bends the fabric of reality, empowering us to manifest our deepest desires."*

— Shree Shambav

### Synopsis

*This section explores the profound meeting point between quantum physics and ancient spiritual traditions, where the invisible forces that shape the universe quietly reveal themselves. The principle of quantum entanglement shows that everything in existence is intricately connected, transcending the barriers of time and distance. Similarly, the observer effect teaches that consciousness is not a passive witness but an active participant—that the mere act of observation influences reality itself.*

*Through this understanding, a new possibility opens: the potential to consciously shape the world we experience. By diving into how focused intentions, thoughts, and awareness interact with the fabric of existence, a deeper truth emerges—we are not separate from creation, but co-creators within it.*

*When we align these quantum principles with our practices of manifestation, we begin to perceive the delicate, luminous threads that weave all of life together. Reality, once seen as fixed and external, is revealed as a living, breathing mirror—one that shifts, responds, and reshapes itself according to the vibration of our inner being.*

*Aarna, her voice steady but filled with wonder, asked, "Guruji, how does the theory of quantum entanglement challenge our conventional understanding of space and time, and how does it support the idea that everything in the universe is interconnected?"*

Guruji, seated in his simple white robe, closed his eyes for a brief moment, as if listening not to the question, but to the silence behind it. Then, opening them slowly, he spoke, his voice both gentle and profound:

"Imagine, Aarna, two seeds planted in different corners of the earth. One grows into a tree in the Himalayas, kissed by snow and wind. The other blooms by the oceans of the south, nourished by salt and sun. To the ordinary eye, they are separate, living independent lives. But if you could see with the eye of deeper truth, you would realise they were once from the same fruit, touched by the same rain, sung to by the same sun. They are forever bound, not by physical proximity, but by a memory older than space and deeper than time.

Quantum entanglement tells us something astonishing: that two particles, once connected, remain connected across any distance. Move one, and the other responds instantly, as if the fabric of space and time is not a barrier but an illusion. It is as if the universe itself remembers their union—and no amount of separation can erase it.

This challenges everything the ordinary mind believes. We think: 'Here' is separate from 'there'. 'Now' is different from 'then'. But entanglement whispers a secret: there is no real separation. Beneath appearances, everything is woven together in a timeless, living tapestry.

You, me, the mountains, the rivers, the stars—we are not isolated islands adrift in a cold, indifferent sea. We are waves of the same vast ocean, dancing, meeting, parting, and reuniting endlessly."

Guruji paused, his eyes shining with the quiet fire of deeper knowing. Then, he continued, offering a story:

"Many years ago, there was a little boy named Kabir, who lived in a village surrounded by dense forests. Every night, before sleeping, he would talk to the stars through his window, believing they listened. His father, a stern man of reason, once told him, 'Stop wasting time. The stars are too far. They don't hear your small voice.' But Kabir never stopped.

One evening, Kabir found a wounded bird beneath a tree. He cared for it with such tenderness that when it finally healed, it would not fly away; it chose to stay. One night, as he whispered his wishes to the stars again, the bird perched beside him and began to sing—an extraordinary, haunting melody.

The villagers, hearing the strange song, said it was the most beautiful thing they had ever heard. Strangers came from distant places just to listen. Kabir smiled silently, knowing the truth: somewhere, somehow, the stars had heard—and sent a song back through the wings of a small bird.

Connection is not bound by logic. It is woven through intention, attention, and love."

Guruji's voice softened even further:

*"The theory of quantum entanglement is the universe's scientific poetry, reminding us:*

*We are not fragments.*

*We are notes of a single, eternal symphony.*

*When you move your heart in kindness, somewhere, unseen, another heart feels it.*

*When you rise in love, the whole cosmos rises a little with you."*

As Guruji's words dissolved into the quiet of Shambav Hall, Aarna sat still, tears glistening quietly in her eyes—not from sadness, but from the overwhelming beauty of realising she had never been, and could never be, alone.

The wind stirred the wildflowers outside, carrying their fragrance inward—a silent confirmation that indeed, everything, everywhere, was listening.

*Dev, his voice a steady ripple in the silence, asked:* "*Guruji, what is the observer effect, and how does it imply that our conscious awareness has a direct influence on the state of the universe, potentially making manifestation possible?*"

Guruji smiled—a slow, knowing smile—and gently placed the small cup of herbal tea in his hand onto the wooden table beside him.

"Dev," he began, "to answer your question, let us step away for a moment from the mind's rigid walls and enter the wide, living field of wonder.

Imagine you are standing before a still pond at dawn. You pick up a pebble and wonder: Will the pond ripple if I do nothing? The water remains silent, mirror-like, until your hand moves, until your intention flows into action. The moment you toss the pebble—whether gently or forcefully—the entire pond responds. It must respond, for it is the nature of the pond to reflect even the smallest gesture.

The observer effect in quantum physics reveals one of the most mind-opening truths about existence: at the most fundamental level of reality—the subatomic level—things don't exist in a fixed, solid state until they are observed.

Imagine this:

Before anyone observes a particle, it is not simply "there" like a pebble lying on the ground. Instead, it exists as a wave of possibilities—a shimmering field of different potential outcomes. It could be here, it could be there, it could spin one way or the other. It exists in a state of pure potential, not locked into any single form.

It is only when consciousness—the act of observation, focused awareness—looks at it, that the particle chooses a position, a spin, a reality. Observation collapses the infinite wave of maybes into one particular experience.

**Let's bring it even closer with an analogy:**

Picture a grand, cosmic orchestra tuning its instruments in a vast concert hall.

There's no set song yet. It's just sounds—a violin here, a soft drum there, a distant flute—a symphony of endless musical possibilities floating in the air.

Now, imagine you, as the conductor, lift your baton.

The moment you *focus* on a particular note, a rhythm, a feeling—the entire orchestra **responds**. The formless sounds *align* themselves into a coherent, beautiful song.

In the same way, before you observe reality, life is this floating symphony of endless maybes, silent music waiting for direction.

*When you observe, when you focus, when you intend—you become the composer.*

*You choose the melody that reality sings.*

Guruji said, "Think of reality like a vast blank canvas—not yet painted, just shimmering with invisible colours. Before you observe it, there are a million different paintings that *could* appear—a sunset, a storm, a forest, an ocean.

But the moment your mind engages—the moment your heart, your consciousness, your focused gaze meets the canvas—the painting begins to form. Not randomly, but *in relationship* to the quality of your attention, your emotion, your expectation."

Guruji, after a pause, said:

- Reality is not fixed.

- You are not a powerless spectator.
- Your conscious awareness literally helps shape the world you experience.

Thus, your thoughts, your feelings, your focus are not just passive experiences inside you—they are creative forces that ripple into the quantum field, shaping what emerges as "real."

**Guruji smiled with a final Whisper:**

*Before you look, life is a mist of dreams.*

*When you look—truly, deeply—you breathe a dream into being.*

Guruji's voice grew softer, drawing them all closer without movement.

"There is a story," Guruji said, "A young seeker named Rivan approached his master and asked, 'Master, why does it seem that sometimes the world changes when I pray, and other times it remains stubborn?'"

The master took Rivan to a field of unopened lotus buds. 'Watch,' he said.

Rivan stared intently at the buds. Hours passed. The sun moved. Still, the buds remained closed.

Frustrated, Rivan said, 'It is useless.'

The master simply smiled and said, 'Look again—not with your eyes, but with your heart.' This time, Rivan softened his gaze, released his impatience, and simply loved the lotuses—without expectation, without force. And slowly, almost imperceptibly, one bud began to unfurl, kissed by an unseen hand.

The master whispered:

*"The universe opens not to those who demand, but to those who truly see."*

Guruji paused, allowing the echo of the story to seep into the hearts around him.

"The observer effect teaches us that our awareness is not passive. It is creative.

Each time you focus on an intention with clarity, love, and trust, you are not merely daydreaming. You are sending ripples into the quantum pond. You are choosing which wave of possibility will rise into form.

However, intention mixed with doubt is like tossing pebbles into the pond and withdrawing your hand halfway. The universe responds to the wholeness of your focus, the purity of your trust.

## The Window of Dreams

Guruji, after a brief pause, said, "Let me narrate another story: In the quiet village of Kumbhariyur, there was a small boy named Arjun who loved to sit by the old, cracked window of his home.

Every evening, after his chores were done, he would rest his chin on the windowsill and simply stare out into the open fields, watching the tall grasses sway like an endless sea.

One day, after a hard rain, the fields were soaked, grey, and heavy with mud. Arjun's elder brother passed by, laughing, "Nothing to see today, just dirt and puddles!" But Arjun stayed, gazing quietly.

He imagined the fields not as ruined, but as brimming with secret life.

In his heart, he saw hidden seeds drinking the rain, sleepy flowers preparing to bloom, earthworms dancing beneath the mud, busy crafting tunnels of life.

As he continued to look—not with boredom, but with love, with wonder, with faith—something began to change.

The next morning, small green shoots had pushed up through the mud. Tiny wildflowers began to bloom where everyone else saw only wreckage.

Villagers said it was just the season. But Arjun knew, somehow, that it had answered his seeing.

He hadn't just watched the world.

He had witnessed it with hope, and in return, life responded.

This is why manifestation is not simply about thinking harder—it is about seeing truer. It is about aligning your inner world with the truth that you are not a separate, powerless creature knocking on the doors of an indifferent cosmos. You are the door. You are the hand that knocks. You are the silent music that invites the door to open."

Dev sat there, his chest rising and falling gently, feeling not just the intellectual understanding of what Guruji said, but sensing a deeper trembling within—the recognition of his own forgotten power.

Outside, as if in agreement, a soft breeze stirred the old banyan tree, scattering a few golden leaves to the earth. No one rushed to speak.

The moment was complete, living, sacred.

*John asked, "Guruji, how can we harness the principles of quantum physics to enhance our manifestation practices, and what are the spiritual parallels to quantum entanglement in ancient traditions?"*

"John," Guruji began, "to harness the principles of quantum physics in manifestation is not to simply intellectualise them—it is to live them, to embody them, to become deeply aware that the universe is not happening to you; it is happening through you."

He paused, letting the silence press gently against the words.

"Quantum physics teaches us that reality, at its most fundamental level, is not made of solid, static matter, but of fluctuating fields of energy and possibility. When you think, when you feel, when you focus with intention, you are not merely reacting to the universe; you are shaping it. You are collapsing possibilities into form."

## The Spiritual Parallel:

Guruji continued, "Thousands of years before quantum theories emerged, seers and mystics spoke of the same truth. In the Vedic tradition, they called it 'Ritam'—the underlying cosmic order that responds to human consciousness. In the Taoist way, it was understood that all things are interconnected through the Tao—an invisible river of being. In Indigenous wisdom across the world, from the Native American to the Aboriginal Australian traditions, there existed a living awareness that thoughts, emotions, and intentions could summon rain, guide harvests, or heal bodies. They understood: The world is not dead matter. It is alive—and you are part of that life."

## The Weaver of Worlds

Guruji's voice grew softer, more intimate, as if sharing a secret across lifetimes.

"Let me tell you a story," he said, and the Hall leaned in, hearts beating in unison.

In an ancient land veiled by mists and memory, there was a woman named Amara, known throughout the villages as the **Weaver of Worlds.**

She owned no loom, no threads, no needles. Her only tools were *her heart, her mind, and her song.*

When a child fell ill, Amara would sit by their bedside and hum softly, weaving threads of hope, health, and light with her voice and intention.

When the fields lay barren after a long drought, Amara would walk among the withered crops, whispering to the earth, her bare feet sinking into the cracked soil. She would **see**—not the desolation—but fields golden with grain, breezes heavy with the scent of ripened fruit.

And without fail, rains would come, crops would flourish, and life would return.

One day, a sceptical traveller asked her, "How can your mind change the earth? You are but one woman against the forces of nature!"

Amara smiled and answered, "The river does not know it is separate from the sea.

When my heart believes in life, life believes in me."

Guruji paused, letting the story settle.

"Amara did not manipulate reality; she harmonised with it. Just as quantum entanglement shows that two particles, once linked, remain connected across time and space, so too, your consciousness is never isolated from the fabric of the universe. When you deeply feel gratitude, hope, love—when you hold a vision not as a desperate wish, but as a living, breathing truth—you are not forcing reality. You are dancing with it."

**Practical Wisdom for Manifestation:**
- **Focus with Heart:** Manifestation is not simply thinking harder; it is *feeling deeper*. Feel the reality you wish to create as if it is already alive within you.

- **Anchor in Stillness:** Just as particles exist in infinite potential before observation, stay rooted in a calm, open state where infinite possibilities can unfold.

- **Release Control:** Trust the unseen orchestration. Entanglement teaches us that connections work beyond logic and visible evidence.

- **Practice Reverence:** Approach life not as a battlefield to conquer, but a sacred web to honour, knowing every thought and feeling sends ripples across existence.

Guruji's voice dropped to a whisper, yet it filled every corner of the Hall:

*"You are not a beggar at the doors of destiny.*

*You are the silent partner in the creation of worlds."*

As the soft breeze stirred the incense smoke into spirals, John closed his eyes, feeling not smaller, but larger—as if his soul had stretched and touched the very edges of the cosmos itself.

The air was rich with the fragrance of sandalwood and wildflowers, and a deep, receptive silence enveloped everyone like a sacred cloak.

*Nita, sitting with quiet intensity, finally broke the hush with her question—one that seemed to ripple through every heart present: "Guruji, in what ways can quantum mechanics explain the power of intention, and how can we apply this knowledge to consciously shape our reality through thought, emotion, and focused energy?"*

Guruji smiled gently, as if he had been patiently waiting for this very moment.

"Nita," Guruji began, "the power of intention is not merely a philosophical idea; it is a cosmic force rooted in the very fabric of existence itself. To understand this, we must first look at what quantum mechanics has shown us."

"At the quantum level," he continued, "reality exists not as solid, predetermined structures but as a field of probabilities—a dance of pure potential. A particle—say an electron—exists not in a single place but everywhere at once, a cloud of possibilities. Only when it is observed—only when consciousness interacts with it—does it collapse into a specific location, a specific state."

"This," Guruji said with a glimmer in his eye, "is the heart of the observer effect: consciousness does not just perceive reality; it chooses it from among infinite possibilities. Your focused attention, your unwavering emotion, your clear intention—these are not passive experiences. They are acts of creation."

### *The Garden That Listened*

Guruji leaned back slightly and spoke in that tender, timeless tone, Let me narrate a story: In a faraway village nestled between emerald hills, there lived a woman named Meera who owned a garden unlike any other. The villagers whispered that Meera's garden bloomed with flowers that no one else could grow—blooms of colours that shifted with the sunlight, fruits that healed sorrow, vines that sang in the rain.

When a curious traveller once asked Meera her secret, she smiled and said simply, *"I speak to the seeds."*

But it wasn't ordinary words.

Every morning, Meera would sit by the freshly sown earth, close her eyes, and feel the fullness of the harvest—not as a hope, not as a distant dream, but as a living truth already alive in her heart.

*She would see the stalks swaying, smell the jasmine in the breeze, and taste the sweetness of the ripe fruits.*

*She would send waves of certainty, gratitude, and love into the soil.*

And the earth, touched by her focused intention, responded. Where others toiled and doubted, Meera co-created. She didn't command the seeds; she aligned with the invisible forces that bring life into being.

"You see, Nita," Guruji said, his voice soft as a prayer, "the universe is like that fertile soil. It does not respond to the mere surface words you utter. It responds to the vibration beneath those words—the clarity of your belief, the fullness of your emotion, the unwavering vision held in your heart."

- **Thought** is like the blueprint.
- **Emotion** is like the life-force energy that waters it.
- **Focused intention** is the sunlight that brings it into form.

When thought, emotion, and energy align without contradiction, manifestation becomes not an effort, but a flowering.

Guruji continued, offering them a sacred path to apply:

- **Clarity of Intention:** Be clear not just about what you want, but why you want it. A scattered mind sends scattered signals.

- **Feel It Now:** Embody the emotional state of already having received. The universe responds to the frequency you emit, not the words you say.

- **Consistent Focus:** Keep returning to your vision, watering it with belief, protecting it from the weeds of doubt.

- **Surrender Timing:** Seeds do not sprout when you demand. They sprout when you trust the invisible rhythms of life.

"Manifestation," Guruji said, "is not about shouting your desires louder. It is about becoming so vibrationally aligned with them that the universe cannot tell where you end and your vision begins."

Nita sat quietly, her hands cupped loosely in her lap, as if already holding the seeds of her future. Something within her shifted—a quiet conviction, a knowing without proof.

*It was not magic.*

*It was not a mystery.*

*It was the most natural thing in the universe.*

*She, too, was the gardener.*
*She, too, could sing reality into bloom.*

Guruji, after a long, thoughtful pause, rose gracefully from his asana. His presence lingered like a fragrance even as he walked quietly across the hall, his hands folded, his steps unhurried. Without a word, the day's session was silently, sacredly concluded.

The devotees, each carrying the weight and wonder of the day's revelations, slowly began to stir. Some remained seated for a moment longer, reluctant to disturb the profound stillness that had settled in their hearts.

Outside Shambav Hall, the universe had painted a masterpiece: the sky glittered with a million stars, shimmering like blessings scattered by unseen hands. Wisps of clouds raced across the heavens, playing an ancient game of hide and seek with the soft, smiling moon. The air was cool and fragrant with the scent of night-blooming jasmine, and a gentle breeze carried whispered prayers across the land.

Some devotees meandered toward the food court to share a simple night's meal; others sought the quiet of the dormitories to refresh themselves. Yet a quiet anticipation hung in the air, as if the night still had more to offer.

## Gathering by the Fire

After dinner, Padma and Nita gathered everyone near the large stone fireplace that stood by the banyan grove. Flames crackled and danced, their golden tongues weaving warmth and light into the cool night.

The devotees, still wrapped in a sacred silence, assembled one by one.

Dev, Vasudeva, and Alice were deep in conversation, voices low but animated, still savouring the day's insights.

It was then that Akshaya gently interrupted the flow of chatter:

"Apeksha wants to share some incidents…" he said, his voice respectful yet carrying a quiet excitement.

A hush fell over the gathering as Apeksha, normally reserved, stepped into the fire's circle of light. Her eyes reflected both vulnerability and courage.

### *The Man Who Carried Stones*

*Apeksha began:*

"During one of Guruji's earlier retreats, a man named Anand came to us. He was a broken man—bitter, angry, carrying years of resentment like heavy stones in his heart. Every small inconvenience enraged him; every word felt like an attack to him."

One afternoon, Anand lashed out during a session, accusing others of being fake, pretending kindness. Many devotees were uncomfortable, unsure how to respond. The air had turned sharp, tense.

But Guruji, with infinite calm, did something none expected.

He walked to the edge of the garden, gathered a handful of large, heavy stones, and brought them to Anand.

Without a word, Guruji handed him the stones and simply said:

*"Carry these with you everywhere you go today."*

Confused but bound by trust, Anand obeyed.

He carried them through meditation, during meals, during walks—his arms aching, his spirit fuming.

By evening, exhausted, Anand collapsed at Guruji's feet, the stones dropping heavily onto the earth.

Tears streaming down his face, he whispered,

*"Why, Guruji? Why this burden?"*

Guruji spoke softly:

"This burden is not mine, Anand. It is yours. You have been carrying invisible stones in your heart for years—stones of anger, of betrayal, of blame. Today, you could feel their weight. Imagine carrying them for a lifetime. You are free to put them down anytime. You only need to choose."

*Anand wept openly that night, releasing not just the stones but years of accumulated pain.*

From that moment on, he changed—becoming one of the gentlest, most compassionate souls many had ever known.

**The Girl Who Could Not Forgive**

Apeksha paused, her voice trembling with emotion, before continuing:

"In another retreat, there was a young woman named Meenal. She had suffered deep betrayals from those closest to her. She wanted to heal but found forgiveness impossible."

During a sacred evening session, Guruji asked her to write a letter—not to her betrayers, but to herself.

"Write," he said, "not from your wounds, but from your wholeness."

Meenal spent hours under the banyan tree, struggling. She wrote with anger, crossed it out. She wrote with sorrow, tore it up.

Finally, somewhere deep in the night, something shifted inside her.

She wrote:

*"I am not what they did to me.*

*I am the love that remained even when the doors were slammed shut.*

*I am the light that flickered, but never went out."*

When she read the letter aloud the next morning, her voice cracked, but it carried the strength of a soul returning home to itself.

Guruji simply placed his hand over her head and said:

*"You have set yourself free. The prison door was never locked. Only you had the key."*

As Apeksha finished speaking, a sacred silence wrapped around the group.

Tears glistened in many eyes, not of sadness, but of deep, soulful recognition.

Each devotee saw a piece of themselves in Anand's burden, in Meenal's battle.

Each felt the invisible weight they, too, were ready to lay down.

The fire crackled gently, as if bearing witness. Above them, the stars continued their ancient vigil, and the moon, shy behind drifting clouds, cast its gentle blessing.

The night stretched long and deep, holding them tenderly in its arms. No one wanted to move, as if breaking the silence would shatter something sacred.

Finally, Kiran rose quietly, his voice barely above a whisper:

"It's time to rest now. Let us carry this light into our dreams."

Slowly, reverently, the group dispersed, each heart carrying a new tenderness, a deeper understanding, and a silent vow to walk a little lighter upon the earth.

After everyone had settled quietly into the embrace of the night, the world outside Shambav Hall grew tender. The stars blinked slowly through the racing clouds, and a cool, knowing breeze wandered through the open windows.

Padma sat by the wide stone window; her face bathed in silver moonlight. She gazed up at the vast sky for a long moment, breathing in its stillness. Then, turning gently to Nita and the others resting nearby, she spoke, her voice barely louder than a whisper.

"Nita... do you remember the reflective meditation Guruji taught us?"

Padma closed her eyes, and with the serene authority of remembrance, she began to guide:

*"Close your eyes.*

*Feel the earth cradling you—timeless, steadfast, and infinitely kind.*

*Breathe in… as if you are sipping the very breath of the stars.*

*Breathe out… and let every burden of the day slip away like leaves upon a river.*

*Now, imagine a soft, golden light hovering just above your head—the light of your truest self—descending gently, like a mother's hand smoothing the hair of her sleeping child.*

*With every breath, allow this light to seep into you.*

*Into your mind, softening every sharp edge of thought.*

*Into your heart, soothing every hidden ache.*

*Into your body, relaxing every fibre worn by the journey.*

*You are not separate. You have never been separate.*

*The stars, the wind, the fire, your breath—all are threads woven through the same great tapestry of Being.*

*Tonight, lay down the stones you have carried—the doubts, the names, the struggles.*

*Lay them down as offerings at the altar of truth.*

*Rest, not as the one who wrestles, but as the one who remembers:*

*You were always free.*

*You were always love.*

*Breathe in this truth.*

*Breathe out everything else."*

After a moment of sacred stillness, Padma softly recited the verse Guruji had once gifted them:

*"I am the breath of the stars,*

*I am the hush of the earth,*

*I am the light between all things.*

*I release.*

*I return.*

*I remember:*

*I am whole."*

The night seemed to listen. A deeper hush wrapped around, as if even the universe was leaning in to hear. And somewhere high above, behind the dance of clouds and moonlight, it felt as if the heavens themselves had smiled—not in grandeur, but in quiet recognition.

# PART TWO

## Reprogramming the Self

*"Every thought you cradle, every emotion you nurture, becomes a thread woven into the silent tapestry of your reality."*

- Shree Shambav

# CHAPTER V

## The Inner Compass

*"The barriers you perceive in life are not the walls of the world, but the limits set by beliefs that have yet to be transformed."*

– Shree Shambav

### Synopsis

Belief systems are the unseen lenses through which we perceive reality and our role within it. They quietly script the stories we live by, shaping not only what we see but what we believe is possible. Our beliefs can either empower the boundless creativity within us or quietly imprison it behind invisible walls.

This section delves into the profound influence of beliefs on the manifestation process, revealing how outdated or limiting patterns can quietly sabotage our deepest aspirations. Through conscious awareness and realignment of these inner frameworks, we reclaim the ability to shape reality with intention and grace.

When belief systems resonate with the natural energy of the universe, manifestation becomes less about effort and more about effortless flow—a co-creation where life responds to the silent music within us. This journey invites the reader to turn inward, to recognise the inner compass they carry, and to reset its direction toward their highest, most expansive potential.

The morning was pleasantly serene. Shambav Hall was alive with quiet energy as devotees moved about, finding their places. A gentle hum of anticipation filled the space. In a few moments, the hall gradually fell into a deep, respectful silence—as if the walls themselves were holding their breath.

Then came the soft, deliberate sound of footsteps approaching. Everyone rose to their feet with reverence, their palms folding in devotion. Guruji entered, his presence calm and radiant, and with a graceful gesture of **Atma Namaste**, he acknowledged the gathering before taking his seat on the asana.

*After the atmosphere settled into a sacred stillness, Lalitha's voice rose, filled with genuine curiosity and innocence, "Guruji, how do belief systems shape the way we experience reality and our ability to manifest?"*

Her question seemed to hang in the air, shimmering like morning light, as all awaited Guruji's response.

Guruji closed his eyes briefly, as if listening to a song only he could hear. The air grew still, dense not with silence, but with meaning ready to unfold.

After a long pause, he spoke, his voice as soft as the breeze:

"Beliefs are the lenses through which you gaze at existence. They are not merely thoughts floating loosely in your mind—they are the architects of your reality, building invisible walls or expansive bridges. Every experience you have, every opportunity you see or miss, every miracle you allow or deny—all are filtered through the architecture of your beliefs."

He let his words sink in, then continued, weaving an analogy:

"Imagine you are born inside a vast, magnificent palace. The palace has thousands of rooms, each filled with wonders—libraries of wisdom, gardens of unimaginable beauty, halls of music and light. But if, from a young age, you are told that only three rooms exist, and that the rest are dangerous or forbidden, you will live your entire life within those three rooms, never knowing the grandeur that lies beyond the doors you were taught not to see."

He paused, his gaze sweeping across the gathered devotees, who were listening with rapt attention.

"Your beliefs are those doors. They determine what rooms of reality you have access to. If your beliefs are small, fearful, or limiting, your life shrinks to fit inside them. If your beliefs are expansive, bold, and full of trust, your reality stretches open—revealing opportunities, connections, and manifestations you would have otherwise missed."

The hall was utterly still. Even the flickering lamps seemed to listen.

**The Boy and the Wall**

Guruji then leaned forward slightly, as if sharing a secret.

"Many years ago, during a retreat in a far-off village, a young boy named Manoj came to me. He was troubled—full of dreams, but convinced he would never achieve them. When I asked why, he said his father had always told him, 'You are not meant for greatness. Stay where you belong.'

This belief had become the wall of his inner palace. Though opportunities knocked at his door, he didn't even hear them because he had already decided they weren't for him.

So I gave Manoj a simple task. I asked him to write down all the things he believed he was 'not allowed' to do. Then, one by one, I asked him to challenge each belief, not with force, but with curiosity: *Is this true? Is this absolutely true? Who would I be without this belief?"*

Guruji smiled gently, the memory warming his face.

"At first, Manoj resisted. He clung to the wall because it felt familiar, even safe. But slowly, as he questioned and released each inherited belief, cracks began to appear. And through those cracks, light poured in.

Within a few years, Manoj became a teacher, a writer, and a guide for others who felt trapped behind walls they didn't even know they had built.

His life didn't transform because the world changed—it transformed because he changed the way he perceived the world."

Guruji let the story linger, like incense trailing into the evening air.

"You see," he said finally, "manifestation is not about forcing the universe to bend to your will. It is about aligning your inner landscape—your beliefs, your emotions, your expectations—with the abundant, expansive nature of reality itself.

When you believe you are limited, you collapse the field of possibilities. When you believe you are limitless, you dance with the infinite."

The sky outside was deepening into velvet night. A few early stars twinkled overhead, as if nodding in agreement.

Lalitha sat in silent wonder, the words etching themselves not just in her mind, but in her very being. She realised then that the walls she thought were outside were always within—and that she held the key.

The morning light poured through the high windows of Shambav Hall, casting a golden glow across the room. The gentle aroma of incense floated in the air, mingling with the stillness that had settled after Lalitha's question.

*As the silence stretched, it was Rohith with a quiet sincerity, he asked, "Guruji, what are the most common limiting beliefs that block successful manifestation, and how can we identify them?"*

Guruji smiled warmly. he leaned forward slightly, his voice deep and calm, weaving a thread of connection to every heart present.

"Rohith," Guruji began, "the most stubborn walls are not built of stone, but of unseen thoughts. These walls live inside us, shaping what we think we can or cannot do. Limiting beliefs are those invisible architects."

He paused, letting the depth of the words sink in.

"There are many forms these beliefs take," Guruji continued. "The fear of failure whispers, 'I will never succeed, so why try?' The shadow of unworthiness says, 'I am not enough to receive love, abundance, or joy.' Scarcity mentality murmurs, 'There's not enough for everyone, and certainly not for me.'"

He looked around the room, his gaze resting briefly on each devotee, making them feel as though he spoke directly to them.

"These beliefs," he said, "are like tinted glasses we do not realise we are wearing. They colour everything we see. No matter how beautiful the landscape, if your lenses are dark, the world will seem dim. If your heart is shackled with fear, the universe's endless offerings will feel out of reach."

Guruji leaned back and began to tell a story: "Many years ago," he said, "there was a young woman named Shambavi. She was bright, kind, and full of dreams—yet always hesitant, always apologising for her existence. She wanted to manifest a fulfilling career in healing arts, but no matter how hard she tried, doors remained closed. She grew frustrated, believing the universe was ignoring her prayers.

One evening, during a quiet session under a vast sky of stars, I asked her to write down the first thought that came to her when she said aloud, 'I am worthy of success.' Tears streamed down her face as she realised her inner voice said, 'No, you're not.'"

Guruji's voice softened even more.

"That tiny voice of doubt—buried deep—was shaping her reality. Not because the universe was cruel, but because she was unknowingly affirming a belief in lack and rejection. The universe, loving and responsive, mirrors what we hold most strongly."

He paused, allowing the story to echo in the silent hall.

"So, how do we find these hidden beliefs?" Guruji asked, smiling gently. "We must become inner archaeologists. When your desire feels far away, ask yourself: What story am I telling myself about why I cannot have this? Write it down. Listen not just with your mind, but with your heart. Patterns will reveal themselves."

**Guruji said to follow a few steps:**

- **Notice resistance**—When something feels hard or impossible, dig deeper into *why*.

- **Trace the roots**—Ask yourself: *Who told me this first? Was it an experience? A parent? Society?*

- **Challenge the old script**—Once exposed, you can choose a new belief: *'I am enough. I am deserving. Abundance is my nature.'*

- **Reaffirm daily**—Healing limiting beliefs is not a one-time act; it is watering a new garden every day with attention, patience, and love.

Guruji ended with a final analogy, his voice weaving a soft tapestry across the hearts in the room:

*"Imagine a bird born inside a cage. Even when the door is opened, if it believes it is meant to live behind bars, it will never fly out. But when it dares to believe in the sky, the entire horizon becomes its home."*

The hall was still, yet alive—every soul stirring inside, awakening, remembering.

*Sujitha raised her hand delicately. Her voice carried both curiosity and an unspoken hope as she asked: "Guruji, in what ways can we realign our belief systems to support manifestation, and how does this shift change our reality?"*

A serene smile crossed Guruji's face, as if Sujitha's question had unlocked a portal to a deeper realm.

He paused for a long moment, allowing the question to ripple across the space, settling into the hearts of every devotee.

Then he spoke, his voice warm and steady:

"Belief systems," Guruji began, "are like the roots of a great tree. The fruits you bear in life—your experiences, your opportunities, your relationships—they all grow from these unseen roots. If the roots are entangled in fear, doubt, and scarcity, the fruits will wither. But when the roots are nourished by trust, love, and infinite possibility, the tree blossoms effortlessly."

He looked around, his eyes shining with a light deeper than words.

"To realign our belief systems," he continued, "we must first become aware of the soil in which they are planted. And then, patiently, tenderly, we must replant."

Guruji then shared a story, drawing everyone even deeper into reflection: "Years ago," Guruji said, "there was a young man named Arun. Arun was brilliant, but he was shackled by a belief that no matter how hard he worked, abundance was always meant for someone else— not him. His father had struggled all his life, and the story of 'life is a battle and loss is inevitable' had been unconsciously passed down like a family heirloom."

"During our sessions," Guruji continued, "I asked Arun to visualise his belief not as a thought, but as a living being. He closed his eyes and saw a small, caged bird, wings folded in fear. Every morning, Arun spent a few moments visualising this bird being set free—the cage door opening, the bird hesitating, then flying into the vastness of the sky. Alongside this, Arun repeated a new affirmation daily: 'Abundance flows to me because I am part of the abundance of life itself.'"

"Slowly but surely, Arun's inner landscape began to change. His career shifted. His relationships deepened. He didn't 'force' manifestation—he became a vessel through which it could naturally flow."

Guruji paused, letting the story breathe into the room.

He then offered practical steps, weaving the teaching with immense clarity:

## 1. Awareness: See the Old Story

- Sit quietly and observe what belief comes up when you think about a dream or desire.
- Is it a belief of hope or a belief of lack?
- Naming the old story is the first step toward liberation.

## 2. Cognitive Reframing: Write a New Script

- Take the limiting belief and reframe it.
- For example, change *"I am not good enough"* to *"I am learning, growing, and becoming more capable every day."*
- Affirm not what you fear, but what you wish to live into.

## 3. Visualisation: Feel the New Reality

- Every day, for a few minutes, imagine yourself living from your new belief.
- Feel it in your body—not just thinking it, but *being* it.
- The subconscious learns through repetition and emotion.

## 4. Affirmations: Speak to Your Roots

- Speak affirmations aloud, not as wishes, but as truths already alive inside you.
- For example: *"I am aligned with the abundance and love of the universe."*

## 5. Compassionate Patience: Growth is Gentle

- Be gentle with yourself.

- Changing beliefs is like teaching an old tree to lean toward the sun. It happens with tenderness, consistency, and trust.

Guruji closed his eyes for a moment, then said with a quiet smile:

"When we realign our beliefs, it is not just our outer life that changes. It is as if the entire universe leans closer to listen, to dance with us, to create with us. The reality we once thought was rigid becomes as fluid as water—ready to take the shape of our highest dreams."

He looked at Sujitha, and then at everyone in the hall.

"You are not here to fight reality," he said. "You are here to remember that you are one with its very fabric. Change your roots, and the whole tree of your life will blossom differently—effortlessly, beautifully, naturally."

Outside, a gentle breeze stirred the leaves, as if the very earth was affirming the truth of Guruji's words.

*Espen, thoughtful and steady, raised his voice, carrying the weight of genuine inquiry: "Guruji, how does the process of belief realignment empower our creative potential and affect our overall well-being?"*

Guruji smiled—a smile that carried both the wisdom of countless journeys and the innocence of a child who still marvels at the stars.

He rose from his asana and slowly walked among the devotees, his bare feet silent against the polished wood. Then he stopped, placed his hands behind his back, and spoke, his voice gentle but carrying the undeniable gravity of truth.

"Beliefs," he began, "are not just thoughts floating in the mind. They are the architects of your internal world. They are the silent sculptors shaping the way your mind perceives, your heart feels, and your body lives."

He paused, letting the words sink deep.

"Imagine your mind as a grand garden. Every belief is a seed planted there. Some seeds grow into flowers that nourish your spirit—courage, love, and abundance. Others, unknowingly sown, become thorns—fear, unworthiness, scarcity. The landscape of this garden determines the fragrance you carry into the world."

Guruji's voice softened even further, weaving a story into the silence: "There was once a woman named Vimala," Guruji said. "From the outside, her life appeared full—a good career, a supportive family. But inside, Vimala was plagued by a silent belief, inherited through years of subtle conditioning: 'I must earn love by being perfect.'"

"This belief was a thorn that wounded her daily, though she never noticed it consciously. It caused her to overwork, to sacrifice her well-being, to fear vulnerability. No matter what she achieved, the inner emptiness grew."

"During a retreat," Guruji continued, "Vimala was guided into a deep reflective meditation where she could finally see this belief—not as her truth, but as a story she had mistaken for truth. With tears streaming down her face, she planted a new seed: 'I am worthy of love simply because I exist.'"

"As days turned into months, something miraculous unfolded. Her health improved; the chronic tension in her shoulders dissolved. Her creativity, once shackled by fear of imperfection, burst forth with vibrancy. New opportunities, deeper relationships, effortless abundance—they flowed into her life, not because she fought harder, but because she aligned herself with the truth of her being."

Guruji closed his eyes briefly, remembering the profound beauty of Vimala's transformation.

Guruji opened his eyes and continued:

**How Belief Realignment Empowers Us:**

**Mental Liberation:**

- When we shift from limiting to empowering beliefs, the mind sheds its chains.
- Instead of seeing barriers, it sees bridges.
- Creativity is no longer a rare spark; it becomes a natural expression.

**Emotional Healing:**

- Old beliefs often carry emotional wounds—fear of rejection, feelings of inadequacy.
- As these beliefs dissolve, emotional resilience and joy arise naturally, like spring after a long winter.

**Physical Well-being:**

- Stress, disease, and fatigue often root themselves in limiting narratives.
- When the belief changes, the body relaxes, the immune system strengthens, and vitality returns.
- Health is not just the absence of illness; it is the harmonious song of mind, body, and spirit in alignment.

**Manifestation Acceleration:**

- Manifestation is not about 'getting' what you want; it's about 'becoming' who you truly are.
- When belief and desire align, the universe responds not out of obligation, but out of resonance.

Guurji held a flower and said:

"See this flower? It does not strive to bloom. It does not wrestle with the soil or doubt its worth. It simply aligns with the sun, the rain, the earth—and blooms by nature of its being."

Guruji smiled. "You, too, are designed to bloom. The only work is to clear the inner soil, to allow the light of truth to reach your roots."

Guruji whispered:

*You are not broken.*

*You are becoming.*

*You are meant to bloom.*

The devotees sat in reverent silence, their hearts swelling not with heavy effort, but with the gentle remembrance of their infinite possibilities.

# CHAPTER VI

## The Invisible Thread

*"Every thought you repeat, every emotion you nurture, quietly lays the bricks of the life you call your own."*

– Shree Shambav

### Synopsis

*Every moment, your thoughts and emotions are silently weaving the fabric of your reality—whether you are aware of it or not. There is a constant, living dialogue between your inner world and the outer world, a conversation too subtle for the hurried mind to hear but powerful enough to shape entire lifetimes.*

*Your beliefs, your focus, and the emotional tones you carry act as architects behind the scenes—influencing your health, your relationships, your opportunities, and even the obstacles you encounter. Nothing is random; everything is a reflection.*

*By becoming aware of this invisible thread—the golden current running between your heart and the universe—you awaken to a deeper truth: you are not merely a participant in life, but its co-creator. When you recognise this, you no longer live by default, shaped by unconscious patterns.*

*You begin to live by design—crafting your reality with purpose, with clarity, and with the quiet power that comes from knowing you are both the dream and the dreamer.*

## Manifestation and Your Life—The Invisible Thread

*Astyn lifted her gaze toward Guruji, her voice carrying a tremor of earnestness. "Guruji, how do unconscious thought patterns influence the reality we experience daily, even when we believe we are not 'manifesting' anything?"*

Guruji's eyes softened. After a long, reflective pause, he spoke: "Astyn, imagine a grand garden, sprawling over hills and valleys. This garden represents your life. Every flower, every thorn, every barren patch was seeded not only by your conscious choices but more often by seeds carried by the unseen winds of your unconscious mind."

"Most people believe they are only planting when they actively make choices—when they intend, when they strive. But the truth is, the garden is always growing. Even when you sleep, even when you are unaware, your deeper mind—your unconscious—is constantly casting seeds into the fertile soil of reality."

"If the unconscious is filled with seeds of fear, self-doubt, scarcity, or unworthiness, those will bloom into patterns of struggle and limitation, without you even realising where they came from. Life appears random, but it is simply responding to what lies beneath the surface."

**Guruji said, "Let me narrate a story."**

"Long ago, in a village nestled between mountains and sea, lived a potter named Arvind. He was known for crafting the finest clay pots—each pot perfectly symmetrical, strong, and beautiful. But strangely, when Arvind tried to make pots for himself—for his own home—they would crack. They would crumble before they could even be fired in the kiln."

"No matter how skilled he was, his own vessels would betray him."

"One night, under a starlit sky, an old monk visited his workshop. Watching Arvind labour in frustration, the monk asked, 'Why do you curse yourself under your breath as you work?' Arvind, startled, replied, 'I do not curse. I barely even speak!'"

"The monk smiled knowingly, 'You do not speak aloud, but your heart mutters all the time: "I am not worthy of fine things. I am only meant to serve others."'"

"It was then Arvind realised—though he never spoke these words, they lived in him, whispering through his hands, shaping the clay, bending his reality to match his inner belief."

"When Arvind worked for others, he poured love, excellence, and generosity. But for himself, the unconscious feeling of unworthiness seeped into every creation. Until he faced this hidden belief, no amount of skill or effort could change the outcome."

**Guruji's voice deepened, carrying a gravity that wrapped around every listener:**

"In the same way, beloved ones, your unconscious thought patterns—the feelings you have normalised, the silent stories you carry—weave the texture of your daily life. Whether you 'try' to manifest or not, you are always manifesting effortlessly, ceaselessly, through the lens of what you hold within."

"To change your outer world, you must first listen inward. You must sit quietly enough to hear the old mutterings beneath the surface. Not with judgment, but with compassion—as a gardener noticing where weeds have grown not by malice, but by long-forgotten seeds."

"Once you see clearly, you have the power to replant. To sow new seeds of worthiness, abundance, love, and infinite possibility."

"Then, without force or struggle, your life will bloom as naturally as the first light of dawn—not because you commanded it, but because you remembered who the true gardener is."

The devotees sat still, their faces calm yet expectant, when Kieron's voice broke the silence—a voice filled with a blend of innocence and earnest seeking.

*"Guruji," Kieron asked, "in what ways can emotional states like fear, gratitude, or joy act as catalysts or barriers to the outcomes we attract into our life?"*

Guruji closed his eyes for a moment, as if reaching into a deeper well of knowing. Then, he opened them, his gaze vast and steady. He began with a story.

"In a small village by the edge of an ancient forest," Guruji said, his voice low and melodic, "there lived two farmers—Karna and Mohan. Both sowed seeds in the same soil, under the same sun, watered by the same rains. Yet when harvest came, Karna's fields flourished with golden wheat, while Mohan's fields bore thin, withered crops.

Curious, the villagers asked the wise elder of the village why such a difference could exist between two neighbours. The elder smiled and said, *'It is not only the seeds and the soil that matter, but the hands and heart that plant them.'*

You see, Karna planted his seeds every morning with a song on his lips, gratitude in his heart, and a vision of abundance so vivid it coloured his every action. Mohan, on the other hand, planted his seeds with fear—fear of drought, fear of pests, fear that he was not worthy of success. His body performed the actions, but his heart wavered, clouded by doubt.

The soil absorbed not just the seeds, but also the vibrations of the sower's emotions."

Guruji paused, letting the story sink into the silence before he continued.

*"Emotions are the energy fields that surround every thought and action,"* he explained. Guruji said, *"They are like the climate in which your inner seeds are planted."*

- **Fear** is like frost—it shrivels potential before it has a chance to bloom. Fear sends a message to the universe that you are not ready, not trusting, not open to receive. Thus, what could have blossomed withers before it even emerges.

- **Gratitude** is the rain—it nourishes unseen roots. Gratitude tells existence that you recognise the abundance already present, creating a magnetic pull for more. The universe responds not to your needs, but to your energy. When you vibrate gratitude, you magnetise greater blessings.
- **Joy** is the sunlight—it energises, amplifies, and accelerates growth. Joy is a pure signal to the cosmos that you are in tune with life's highest frequencies. Manifestation becomes effortless when joy flows, because you are not reaching for life—you are dancing with it.

Guruji leaned forward slightly, his eyes soft yet piercing.

**"Most people think manifestation begins with asking. It doesn't. It begins with being."**

Guurji continued, "If your emotional state is clouded by chronic fear, resentment, or unworthiness, no matter what you ask for, the energy you emit will repel it. It's like tuning into a radio station but broadcasting on the wrong frequency. You might pray for love, but if you feel unlovable deep inside, you block its arrival."

He then shared a simple yet profound practice: *"Every morning, before speaking a single word, feel three things you are grateful for. Every night, before sleep, offer three joys you experienced that day to the sky. Gratitude and joy, practised daily, will till the soil of your inner world until miracles grow like wildflowers."*

Kieron sat in a quiet awe, as if his heart had received more than an answer—it had received a key.

*Martina, after a pause, her voice trembling with a mixture of vulnerability and hope, asked, "Guruji, how can becoming aware of our 'default mindset'—the beliefs and emotions we dwell in most—help us realign with the life we truly want to create?"*

Guruji closed his eyes for a few moments, as if drinking deeply from the silence within. When he opened them, his gaze was warm, his voice a soft, flowing river.

Guruji said, "Once, there was a young sculptor named Veeran who sought to carve the most magnificent statue his village had ever seen. Day after day, he chipped away at the stone, but no matter how hard he worked, the figure emerging was rough, imbalanced, and unlike the vision he held in his heart.

Disheartened, he approached the village elder and pleaded, 'I have the finest stone, the sharpest tools, and the clearest image in my mind. Why does my creation not reflect my dream?'

The elder smiled and led him to a still pond. 'Throw a stone into the water,' he instructed.

Veeran did, and ripples distorted the surface.

'Now, look into the water and try to see your reflection,' the elder said.

Veeran peered, but all he could see was a broken, shifting image.

The elder said gently, 'When your inner world is rippled with unconscious fear, doubt, and unworthiness, your outer creation will always come out distorted, no matter your tools or dreams. First, calm the waters.'"

Guruji's words drifted into the silence like a sacred offering.

He turned to the gathering and said, "Your default mindset is the water from which your entire reality reflects."

Guruji continued with deeper emotion:

"Most of us are trying to 'build' a new life, a new dream, without ever checking the state of the waters inside us. If we wake up each day tangled in habitual fear or swim unconsciously in currents of scarcity, resentment, or self-doubt, then no matter how beautiful our dreams, they will reflect the turbulence, not the dream itself.

Becoming aware of your default mindset is like sitting by the pond of your own being and noticing—with great honesty and compassion—whether the water is still, stormy, or poisoned with old griefs and expectations."

Guruji paused, letting the weight of those words settle into every heart present.

He went on, offering the path forward:

- **Awareness is the first light**—Before change can happen, you must see what you are swimming in.
- **Acceptance is the soft soil**—Do not shame yourself for the turbulence. Love it, for it has carried you this far.

- **Conscious Choice is the sculptor's hand**—Each day, each moment, choose emotions and beliefs that align with your soul's true vision: beliefs of worthiness, trust, expansion, and gratitude.

Guruji leaned forward slightly, his voice lowering as if sharing a sacred secret:

"The universe does not respond only to your desires. It responds to the vibration of your being. Change your dominant emotional climate, and your life rearranges itself like a forest after rain."

Then, Guruji shared a simple practice, filled with tenderness:

### The Mirror Practice

*"Each morning, before you face the world, face yourself. Look into your eyes and say with deep conviction: 'I am worthy of my dreams. I am capable of receiving. I am the calm water where miracles can be reflected.'"*

The devotees sat spellbound, many with tears shining in their eyes, feeling an inner doorway creak open.

Martina pressed her hands to her heart, overwhelmed with gratitude.

She realised it wasn't about fighting the world outside; it was about becoming the loving guardian of the world within.

Guruji whispered:

***Change your inner sky, and the constellations of your life will shift.***

*Greta's voice rose, tender but strong, "Guruji, what practices can we adopt to consciously shift our inner world so our outer world begins to mirror the reality we desire?"*

Guruji smiled warmly, as if Greta's question was a long-lost melody finally finding its way home.

He folded his hands together and began:

"Imagine your life as a grand, ancient tree.

The fruits it bears—sweet or bitter—are not random. They are born of the seeds you planted long ago in the soil of your inner world. If you desire different fruits, you must tend to the roots."

He paused, his gaze sweeping across the attentive faces.

"Most people," he continued, "focus on changing the fruits—struggling with circumstances, outcomes, appearances—without ever reaching down into the soil where the real power lies: their thoughts, beliefs, and emotional patterns."

He shifted forward slightly, as if leaning into the heart of the conversation:

"Your inner world is the loom. Your emotions, beliefs, and thoughts are the threads.

Each day, you are weaving the tapestry of your tomorrow—stitch by invisible stitch."

Guruji, after a pause, said, "Let us understand this sacred map, to tend this inner garden:

## 1. Daily Awareness Rituals

"Morning is when the veil is thinnest," he said softly.

Before the world's noise floods you, sit for five minutes and tune into your emotional weather.

Are you beginning with gratitude or with resentment? With fear or with wonder?

Notice. Name it. No judgment. Awareness alone loosens the grip of old patterns.

## 2. Emotional Alchemy

Guruji said, "Every emotion is a messenger."

Instead of resisting or suppressing 'negative' emotions, breathe into them.

Ask them, gently, 'What are you trying to teach me?'

Fear may be a guardian of forgotten dreams. Anger may be a mask of sadness.

Listening transforms pain into power.

## 3. Affirmation as Reprogramming

"Words are spells you cast upon yourself," Guruji said, voice deepening.

Each morning and night, whisper to your soul words that weave a new reality:

*'I am enough.'*

*'I am open to miracles.'*

*'My life blooms with grace.'*

Feel the emotion behind the words—emotion is the ink that writes reality.

### 4. Visualisation—The Art of Inner Seeing

Guruji smiled, eyes twinkling,

"The universe responds to pictures painted in the heart, not just wishes muttered by the lips."

Before sleep, close your eyes and feel yourself already living your desired life.

Taste it. Touch it. Walk inside it in your imagination. Emotionally inhabit the future you wish to create.

### 5. Service and Compassion

"Love is the most powerful vibration," Guruji said.

"When you bless others' journeys, when you lift others without seeking reward, you open a gateway for blessings to flow effortlessly into your own life."

Even a small act of kindness resets the magnetic field of your being.

Guruji's voice softened even more, becoming almost a whisper wrapped in starlight:

*"The inner world shifts not through force, but through tenderness. Not through striving, but through surrender to a greater wisdom already alive within you."*

Guruji leaned back, after a pause, said, "Let me narrate a story: Long ago, there was a weaver who spent her whole life trying to create the perfect tapestry.

She tried new colours, stronger threads, faster hands—yet the fabric always tore or dulled.

In despair, she went to a wise elder, who said, 'Child, the problem is not your threads.

It is the place where you sit—it is soaked in sorrow, bitterness, and fear.

Move to higher ground. Weave where the air is clear, where the sun kisses the earth.

Then your tapestries will sing.'

The weaver moved.

And her creations became so beautiful that even the heavens bent low to admire them."

The hall was silent, filled with the golden weight of truth.

Greta pressed her palms together, bowing deeply, her heart swelling with a new kind of knowing:

*The work was never outside. It was always within.*

Guruji whispered:

*Weave well, dear soul. Your masterpiece is waiting.*

The morning air was filled with a tender freshness, like the world itself had just taken a long, cleansing breath. Leaves shimmered under the gentle sun. Birds flitted from branch to branch, their songs weaving an invisible music through the grounds of Shambav Ashram.

After the intense morning session, Guruji had asked everyone to take a brief break—to walk, to breathe, to simply be. The devotees, still wrapped in the lingering energy of the teachings, moved quietly, savouring steaming cups of herbal tea brewed with Tulsi, lemongrass, and rose petals.

Padma, Akshaya, Vasudeva, and a few others ambled along the stone pathways that meandered through the gardens. The gravel crunched under their sandals as they strolled slowly, conversations flowing in gentle murmurs.

It was then that Sofia, her eyes sparkling with curiosity, interrupted the easy rhythm of the walk and said, "Apeksha, share some interesting story… something we haven't heard yet!"

Everyone turned towards Apeksha, who was sipping her tea thoughtfully.

Akshaya chuckled and added warmly, "Yes, yes—Apeksha is a walking treasure chest of stories and wisdom!"

Laughter bubbled up among them, light and genuine, lifting the already vibrant morning higher.

Apeksha smiled, a knowing, almost mischievous smile, and after a long pause—as if pulling a memory from deep within her heart—she said,

*"Do you see that large rock boulder over there, resting at the edge of the grove?"*

Everyone turned to look. It was an ancient, weathered stone, half-covered in moss, silent and strong as though it had witnessed the passing of countless ages.

"Let me tell you an incident," Apeksha began, her voice soft but clear, carrying the gravity of what was to come. "And more importantly, let me share how Guruji reflected on it… and what we learned that day."

"It was many years ago," she said, "during another retreat, when a few of us were walking the grounds after a storm. The earth was slick with rain, and some of the paths were difficult to tread. Near that very boulder, one of the younger devotees, Hari, slipped and twisted his ankle badly. He cried out in pain, frustrated and embarrassed."

"We rushed to help him, of course. But Guruji, who was walking just a little behind us, approached calmly. He didn't immediately attend to Hari's injury. Instead, he stood before the massive stone and laid his hand upon it."

"He said, 'This rock has stood here for perhaps hundreds of years. It has endured storms, scorching heat, relentless rains, and the passing footsteps of countless souls. Yet it does not complain. It simply is—strong, steady, patient.'"

Apeksha's voice softened, growing tender:

"Guruji turned to Hari, who was gritting his teeth against the pain, and said, 'Pain is like the rain, like the storm. It is not your enemy. It comes, sometimes harshly, to carve away what is brittle in you, to reveal what is enduring. Your spirit is the rock, Hari. Not the wound, not the stumble.'

'Attend to your pain,' Guruji said, 'but remember your essence. Be the rock.'"

The group around Apeksha was silent now, breathing in her every word, feeling the truth vibrating within them.

"Later," Apeksha continued, "Guruji shared with us that life would always bring falls, heartbreaks, sudden storms—but that what defines us is not the fall itself, nor the immediate pain… but the remembering of our deeper nature. The unmoving, unshakable core within."

She looked toward the boulder again, her eyes misty.

"That day," she whispered, "we didn't just help Hari heal his ankle. We each touched a part of ourselves that could never be broken."

Just then, the distant chime of the Shambav Hall bell echoed through the air—a sound as soft and certain as a heartbeat, calling everyone back to the sacred space.

The group stirred gently, almost reluctant to break the sacred moment. They walked in silence toward the hall, the image of the rock—and the truth it symbolised—quietly rooting itself inside each of them.

The day's lessons were not only written in words or lectures, but etched into the living moments—in stones, in storms, in the spaces between heartbeats.

*The journey continued.*

# CHAPTER VII

## The Soul's Cosmic Library

*"Your destiny is not written in stone, but in vibration—the Akashic Records whisper the design, and your heart completes the blueprint."*

– Shree Shambav

### Synopsis

*Beyond the physical world lies a subtle, infinite archive known as the Akashic Records—a dimension where every thought, intention, and action, past, present, or future, is lovingly preserved. Accessing this cosmic library offers a profound opportunity: to glimpse your soul's original blueprint, to uncover hidden patterns that silently shape your life, and to reconnect with the deeper currents of your true purpose.*

*When desires are rooted in the wisdom held within these universal records, manifestation moves from scattered effort to sacred precision. Instead of drifting through life, reacting to each wave, you begin to consciously co-create with existence itself—weaving a reality that is not only aligned with your dreams but also with the timeless calling of your soul.*

### The Akashic Records—The Soul's Cosmic Library

*Abhilasha's voice was soft, but full of wonder:* "Guruji, how do the Akashic Records influence the manifestation of events in our present life, *and what role does awareness of past experiences play in shaping new realities?"*

Guruji opened his eyes slowly, his gaze meeting hers with deep warmth. "Ah, Abhilasha," he began, "you ask not just a question, but summon a memory of the soul."

### The Garden of Invisible Seeds

"Imagine your life as a vast garden," Guruji said, "but one that didn't begin when you were born. Long before you took your first breath, seeds were sown—some by your own soul's previous intentions, and others through lifetimes of experience, choices, emotions, and learning. The Akashic Records are like the soil of this garden. They contain every seed, every storm, every bloom—the entire ecosystem of your soul's journey. Nothing is lost there. Nothing is erased. All is remembered, in love and clarity.

But here is what matters most: those records are not meant to imprison you. They are not ledgers of karma to bind you. They are sacred mirrors—offered so you may see clearly what needs healing, what asks to be honoured, and what longs to be transformed."

### The Wounded Sculptor:

Guruji paused, let me narrate a story: "There was once a woman named Amrita who came to the retreat years ago. She was a brilliant sculptor but lived in deep fear. No matter how much success she tasted, something inside always sabotaged her. She would abandon projects, push away love, and live in chronic pain, as if punished by something invisible.

During one session, as we entered deep Akashic reflection, a memory surfaced. Not from this life, but from another. In that life, Amrita had been an artist too, but was persecuted for speaking the truth through her work. Her soul had carried forward that imprint—that 'if I express my gift fully, I will suffer.' And though she couldn't logically explain why, her present life was shaped by this unseen wound.

When she saw it, truly saw it—not as superstition, but as soul memory—she wept. Not out of fear, but out of *relief*. It was no longer a curse. It was a pattern, one that could be acknowledged, honoured, and released. She began sculpting again. Not out of fear, but joy. Her pain eased. Her relationships healed. *She rewrote the contract.*"

## The Role of Awareness in Manifestation

"Awareness," Guruji said slowly, "is the key to the Akashic gate. When you bring light to a shadow—whether it's an old belief, a traumatic echo, or a fear inherited across time—it loses its power to unconsciously steer your life. The universe responds not just to what you want, but to what you carry beneath your want.

So, when you become aware of the records—when you ask, *'What deeper truth is this pattern pointing to?'*—you no longer manifest out of old wounds. You manifest out of a new alignment. That's when true creation begins."

"Think of a river," Guruji continued. "You see the surface current—fast, rushing, visible. That's your daily life, your conscious desires. But underneath is a deeper current— shaped by unseen terrain, by rocks and caves and bends laid down long ago. That's your Akashic imprint. Unless you dive into that deeper current, you may never understand why your life keeps flowing in a certain direction.

But when you do? You can reroute it. Not by fighting the river… but by reshaping its bed with conscious love and awareness."

Silence settled like a gentle mist. Abhilasha wiped a tear from her cheek. She was not alone. Many eyes glistened—not from sorrow, but from recognition. Something in them had been remembered.

Guruji softly said, "Your soul is not a prisoner of the past. It is a bridge between what was, what is, and what still can be. The Akashic Records are not just a library—they are an invitation. To remember. To release. To rise."

*"Guruji," Akanksh asked, "can accessing the Akashic Records help identify emotional and mental blocks that hinder manifestation, and if so—how does this process lead to clarity and transformation?"*

**The Mirror in the Attic**

"Akanksh," Guruji began, "imagine a large ancestral home. You've lived there your whole life, using the same few rooms every day. But hidden above is an attic, locked and dusty. You've heard whispers about it but never dared to enter.

One day, you find the key and ascend the creaking staircase. As the door swings open, you're met with objects wrapped in cloth, old letters, half-faded portraits, and journals scribbled in forgotten languages.

This attic is your **Akashic imprint**—the part of your consciousness that has stored not just memories from this life, but karmic impressions, soul agreements, ancestral wounds, and emotional residues carried across time. Not all are dark. Some are luminous, filled with gifts you've forgotten. But some are tangled—holding grief, shame, fear, or beliefs that no longer serve your soul's evolution."

**A Story of a Blocked Voice**

Guruji said, "Let me share a story. There was a seeker named Rhea who once came to me, unable to manifest what she most longed for: to be a teacher and speaker. Every time she stood before others, her voice would tremble, her thoughts scatter, and her body freeze.

She thought it was just stage fright. But the fear was disproportionate. So I guided her into the Akashic field through deep stillness, intention, and sacred inquiry.

There, an image arose—of a life centuries ago, where she had been a truth-teller, a spiritual woman who dared to speak out against injustice in her village. For doing so, she was silenced—violently. That trauma had buried itself deep in her soul's memory, shaping her belief: **'If I speak, I will suffer.'**

In this life, she had no memory of that— but the fear ruled her anyway. It wasn't just a personal insecurity. It was a soul memory waiting to be seen."

## Bringing Light into the Archive

"When she saw it," Guruji continued, "not as fantasy, but with the emotional clarity and tears of recognition, she understood. And in that understanding, she forgave. Not just those who hurt her… but the part of herself that had stayed small for so long.

From that moment on, her voice began to return. Not all at once. But something had shifted at the roots. She began speaking to small groups, then larger ones. And the joy returned, because the fear no longer ruled her subconscious."

## The Dam and the River

"Imagine manifestation as a river," Guruji said. "Your desires are the current. Your thoughts are the stones guiding their flow. But your **unseen emotional blocks**? They are the dam.

You may shout affirmations. You may set intentions. But if there is a block—deep and hidden, built on fear or shame or inherited belief, the river cannot flow.

Accessing the Akashic Records is like diving beneath the surface, finding the dam, understanding why it was built, and then—not tearing it down in anger—but gently removing each stone with awareness and love.

The moment the dam is gone, the river doesn't need to be told where to go. It *remembers*. It flows with its intelligence."

## The Path to Clarity and Transformation

"To access these records," Guruji continued, "you don't need to be a mystic or psychic. You need to be **willing to listen—**

deeply and humbly—to the parts of yourself that have been left behind. Ask yourself:

- What patterns keep repeating?
- Where do I sabotage my own joy?
- What am I afraid will happen if I succeed?

These questions are doors. Sit with them in stillness, journal them, invite your soul to show you. Dreams, intuitions, even conversations with others will begin to bring the answers."

Guruji's voice grew softer, "Akanksh… the Akashic Records are not a fantasy realm. They are the *unspoken wisdom* inside you, waiting to be reclaimed. When you look at your emotional and mental blocks through the lens of this ancient memory, what once seemed like weakness becomes your greatest doorway to truth.

And when that happens— manifestation is no longer about struggle. It becomes remembrance. Alignment. Grace."

A hush fell upon the circle.

Somewhere nearby, a bird called out—as if affirming the silence that followed had already answered the next unasked question.

It was Akshatha who gently broke the silence, her voice neither hesitant nor bold, but reverent—like a bell rung not to shatter the stillness, but to bless it.

*"Guruji,"* she asked, *"in what ways can tuning into the Akashic Records align personal desires with the greater flow of universal purpose?"*

### The River and the Sky

"Akshatha," Guruji began gently, "imagine a river born in the cradle of the mountains. In its early journey, it is restless. It crashes over stones, carves through valleys, erodes cliffs—convinced that the only way forward is by force. It believes its destination must be achieved, earned through struggle.

But high above it floats the sky—silent, endless, unbound—watching not just the river's present, but its origin and its end.

If the river could pause for even a moment and reflect the sky—truly *see* itself in that vast stillness, something within it would shift. It would no longer struggle blindly. It would begin to flow… not with resistance, but with grace. Not from surrender, but from understanding."

He paused, letting the silence cradle his words like a mother holds a newborn.

"The **Akashic Records** are like that sky. They do not impose a path upon you—they *illuminate* it. They are the sacred memory of your soul, etched across lifetimes. They contain the essence of who you are, why you came, and what echoes through your heart in this life—even when the world tries to drown that voice."

### The Song Remembered

Guruji's eyes momentarily wandered to the great bronze bell at the rear of the hall. "There was once a young man, Aditya, who came here years ago. As a child, music was his first language. He heard rhythm in rain, harmony in birdsong, and melody in the silence between two heartbeats. His soul didn't *learn* music—it *remembered* it."

"But life, as it often does, demanded he be 'practical.' So he pursued commerce, built enterprises, and won respect. On the outside, he succeeded. But within, he starved."

"By the time he arrived here, he was not broken—he was buried."

Guruji's voice softened, like the whisper of an old prayer.

"Through reflection and meditation, Aditya accessed the Akashic field—not as mysticism, but as memory. He uncovered lifetimes where music was his dharma: as a temple singer who carried devotion in song… a tribal flute-carrier whose notes healed sorrow… a mystic bard who turned pain into poetry."

"The ache he felt in this life was not confusion—it was *remembrance*. His soul wasn't lost… it was homesick."

"When he realigned with that thread—when he honoured not what was expected, but what was *eternal* in him—life opened. Not because the world changed, but because he did. Music returned not as a profession, but as a purpose. His art became an offering. His performance became prayer. This is what happens when we walk in rhythm with our soul's design."

## The Seed Within

Guruji placed his hand gently on his chest, as if touching a truth too sacred for words.

"True desires are not loud. They whisper. They come not from the ego's hunger, but from the soul's memory. The **Akashic Records** help you remember the seed planted within you before you were born—the seed you came here to water."

"They are not a fortune-telling book. They are a frequency, a mirror of your soul's intention. When you attune to them, you don't escape life—you *enter it fully*, but now with clarity, alignment, and love."

"Every real desire is not a detour—it is a compass. It does not pull you away from the Divine. It points you *toward it*."

He looked around the room—eyes glistening, not with emotion, but with stillness deeper than tears.

"When your desires are aligned with your soul's song, the universe doesn't resist you. It *joins you*. What you attract is no longer effort—it is **entrusted** to you."

A sense of timelessness filled Shambav Hall, as if past and present were gently folding into one. It was Apeksha who spoke next. Her voice was steady, but there was something more in her tone—a longing not just for knowledge, but for the kind of truth that reshapes a life.

*"Guruji," she asked, "how do the Akashic Records reveal the interconnectedness of thoughts, actions, and outcomes across lifetimes—*

*and how can this awareness enhance conscious manifestation in the present?"*

## The Loom of Lives

"Apeksha," Guruji began softly, "imagine a weaver sitting before a vast loom—not weaving a single garment, but a tapestry of lifetimes. Each thread represents a thought. Each knot, an action. Each colour, an intention. You may only see the part in front of you—the life you now live—but behind the veil lies an intricate pattern formed by every lifetime before this one."

He paused, his voice deepening.

"The Akashic Records are the loom's master design—the cosmic memory where the threads of cause and effect, karma and grace, are recorded. They do not judge. They simply remember."

Guruji said, "Let me narrate a story: There was once a woman named Shanta, who lived in a quiet village near Rishikesh. From a young age, she experienced an unexplained sadness—as if something within her had been left undone, but she could not name it. She had dreams of water she had never seen, melodies she had never sung, and a sense of guilt that had no source in her present life."

"Through deep meditation and Akashic insight, she remembered a lifetime where she was a monk in ancient Nalanda. In that life, she was a scribe who had access to sacred teachings. But in her fear of persecution, she had hidden many of those truths rather than share them. Her soul had carried that remorse across incarnations—the regret of a voice silenced."

"Now, in this life, she was a teacher. And when she finally understood the *interconnection*, the reason for her longing and hesitation—something inside her unlocked. She began teaching not just facts, but wisdom. Not just curriculum, but consciousness."

Guruji looked across the room, his voice luminous.

"Awareness of the **Akashic field** does not burden us with past sins. It *frees* us by showing us the *continuity of intention*. The tears we cry now may be echoes of ancient joys deferred… or promises made to ourselves long ago. When we understand this, we begin to *manifest consciously*—not out of fear or lack, but with remembrance and alignment."

**The Garden of the Soul**

"Imagine," Guruji continued, "your soul as a **garden**. In one lifetime, you plant seeds. In another, you water them. Next, you may clear weeds or feel the shade of a tree you do not remember planting. The Akashic Records allow you to walk through this garden—to see the entire ecosystem of your being, not just the flower blooming today."

"When we access this garden, we begin to manifest with *clarity*, not confusion. We ask not 'What do I want?' but 'What is seeking to emerge through me that has always been mine?'"

*Guruji then lifted his gaze gently, as if looking not merely to the sky, but beyond it—into the memory of the cosmos itself.*

"The **Akashic Field**," he said, "though it carries different names across traditions, is not a modern invention. It is the *ancient memory*—the silent witness—that has echoed through the spiritual hearts of all great traditions. It is not always described as a 'record', but it is always known as *that which remembers all.*"

### Hinduism—Akasha & Chidakasha

"In **Hindu Dharma**, the **Akasha** is one of the *Panchamahabhutas*—the five great elements: earth (*prithvi*), water (*apah*), fire (*agni*), air (*vayu*), and ether (*akasha*). Among these, **Akasha** is the subtlest—the field of pure potential where sound, thought, and karma are held."

- **Chandogya Upanishad** (7.12.1): *"Akasha is greater than fire. For in Akasha indeed all things are born, and into Akasha they merge at the end."*

- **Yoga Vashistha**, in the chapter on Chidakasha, speaks of *"Chidakasha"*—the **sky of consciousness**, where the impressions (*vasanas*) of all actions and thoughts dwell. It is said:

*"All the worlds exist in the infinite consciousness like fruits in a basket."* (Yoga Vashistha, Nirvana Prakarana)

Thus, Akasha here is not just space, but a conscious, eternal witness—a field of remembrance where all karmic seeds are stored.

## Buddhism:

## Ālaya-Vijñāna Storehouse Consciousness

"In Mahayana and Yogācāra Buddhism, particularly in the Tibetan tradition, the concept of the Ālaya-Vijñāna or 'Storehouse Consciousness' closely mirrors the Akashic idea."

- **Lankavatara Sutra**, a core Yogācāra text:

*"Ālaya-vijñāna is the base of all operations of the mind. It stores all karmic impressions like seeds, and these seeds ripen into experience."*

This *Ālaya*, also called the eighth consciousness, is seen as the container of all karmic imprints, forming the foundation of rebirth and continuity.

## Christianity—The Book of Life

"In the Christian tradition, particularly in the Book of Revelation, there is a reference to the **Book of Life**, a divine record that holds every soul's action and intention."

- **Revelation 20:12**:

*"And I saw the dead, small and great, stand before God; and the books were opened: and another book was opened, which is the Book of Life: and the dead were judged out of those things which were written in the books, according to their works."*

Here, the Book of Life functions as a sacred ledger—a divine Akashic record—showing the cause-effect continuity and the moral accounting of souls.

## Sufism—Lauh-e-Mahfuz (The Preserved Tablet)

"In **Islamic mysticism**, especially in **Sufism**, the concept of the **Lauh-e-Mahfuz** or *Preserved Tablet* refers to a metaphysical reality where all divine decrees and soul-journeys are inscribed."

- **Qur'an**, Surah Al-Buruj (85:21-22):

*"Nay! This is a glorious Qur'an, inscribed in a Preserved Tablet."*

Rumi, in his poetic vision, echoes this:

*"There is a tablet in the heavens, upon which all things are written—every breath, every sigh."* - Rumi's *Masnavi*, Book IV

This Tablet holds the soul's journey—not as punishment or reward—but as the unfolding of divine will and remembrance.

### Taoism—Tao as the Field of Memory

"In **Taoism**, while the language of 'records' is absent, the Tao itself represents the primordial order, the pattern of reality that holds the memory of all transformations."

- **Tao Te Ching**, Chapter 2 (translated by Gia-Fu Feng):

*"Being and non-being create each other. Difficult and easy support each other... before and after follow each other."*

In this view, the Tao is the **undivided field** of potential and pattern—the *Akasha before name*—and tuning into it is tuning into the eternal unfolding.

## Jainism—Lesya, Lokakash, and Karmic Particles

"In **Jainism**, the Akashic field appears as the **Lokakash**—the space in which all beings and karmic particles exist. Each soul is surrounded by **karmic matter**, and the quality of one's thoughts (*Lesya*) determines the colour and density of this aura."

- **Tattvartha Sutra** (Chapter 2):

*"The soul and karmic matter interact through vibrations. Karma binds to the soul due to passions."*

- **Lesya's theory** explains how past intentions and thoughts influence the current state of consciousness and perception—offering a vivid Akashic parallel.

Guruji's voice lowered, but it carried the intensity of lifetimes:

"Across these great traditions, we see the same truth: that our actions, thoughts, and even longings are not lost. They are remembered—not by God as a judge, but by the **Universe as a witness**. The Akashic field, or whatever name you give it, is the silent soul-memory of all that is."

"When we align with it, we don't predict our future—we remember what was always encoded within us. And that remembrance," he smiled, "is the beginning of freedom."

## Manifesting Through Sacred Memory

"To consciously manifest is not to manipulate reality," Guruji said. "It is to harmonise with your soul's original intent—the intent planted across lifetimes. The Akashic Records are not there to bind you to the past. They are there to remind you of what you came here to *complete*, to *redeem*, to *become*."

He folded his hands gently.

"When you remember who you've been, you understand more deeply who you are—and from that place, your manifestations become not wishes… but echoes of destiny awakening into form."

After a long and contemplative pause, Guruji gently folded his hands and smiled, his eyes resting briefly on each devotee before him.

"Let us now break for the midday meal," he said warmly. "Nourish your body as you have nourished your spirit this morning."

The devotees slowly began rising from their seats inside Shambav Hall, the hush of the discourse still lingering like incense in the air. Some moved toward the food mall, while others walked quietly beneath the open sky, the sounds of birdsong and rustling leaves returning to the foreground.

Under the soft golden light, Padma, Nita, and Vasudeva paused near the steps and turned to the others.

"Let's meet under the Banyan tree after lunch," Padma suggested.
"Yes," Nita added, "It will be the perfect place to reflect and share."

After a delicious and soul-satisfying meal, everyone slowly made their way to the ancient **Banyan tree**, whose sprawling roots and wide canopy had long offered shelter not just from the sun—but from restlessness.

In its sacred shade, Nita, Lalitha, Rohith, and Sujitha sat cross-legged in a loose circle, animated in gentle conversation. Their voices rose and fell like birds gliding on morning thermals, discussing the morning session—its stories, its metaphors, and the way Guruji's words seemed to pierce gently, yet precisely, into their inner lives.

The golden afternoon sunlight filtered through the thick, drooping arms of the ancient Banyan tree, casting a soft mosaic of shadows on the earth. The air was calm, almost reverent—as though even the breeze paused to listen.

Martina's voice broke the gentle murmurs, her tone eager and tender:

"Apeksha… why don't you narrate some incident? Your way of telling… it touches the heart. It brings clarity."

There was a silence, not of awkwardness, but of stillness.

Akshaya smiled, and so did the others—knowing well that when Apeksha spoke, time often softened its grip.

Apeksha looked toward the old Banyan roots, as if drawing memory from the very soil beneath them. After a breath, she began:

## The Girl Who Feared Her Own Voice

"Many years ago," she said, "a young woman named Sneha came to the Ashram. She barely spoke. Not out of humility—but fear. Every time she tried to express herself, a tremor ran through her. Her voice would break. She thought something was wrong with her."

Sneha had grown up in a family where silence was mistaken for respect, and questions were seen as rebellion. By the time she reached her twenties, she had learned to erase herself gently from every room.

"One evening," Apeksha continued, "during a satsang like this, Guruji asked everyone to chant their soul's sound—not a mantra, but a vibration that *felt true*. When it was Sneha's turn, she froze. Her lips trembled. Tears welled up. She whispered, *'I have no sound.'*"

Guruji didn't respond immediately. He simply picked up a **silent tanpura** beside him—untouched for years. With his fingers, he *plucked the string*, and a deep hum filled the air.

"This sound," he said, "was always in the tanpura. But it needed someone to trust it enough to touch it."

That night, Sneha sat under this very Banyan tree and wept—not out of grief, but release. Over the next weeks, she began humming, then speaking, then singing. Her voice became a river. Today, she teaches music therapy to children who have lost speech through trauma.

"The learning?" Apeksha said softly, "Your soul has a voice. Silence is sacred, yes. But fear is not. What you do not express becomes the burden you carry."

## The Monk Who Couldn't Forgive

Apeksha paused and let the rustle of leaves fill the space. Then she looked at Lalitha and continued:

"Another time, an elderly seeker named Mahadev arrived. He wore ochre robes. He had studied the Gita, the Vedas, and all the commentaries. But one afternoon, during darshan, he confessed—*'I have mastered many things, Guruji... except forgiveness.'*"

His brother had betrayed him decades ago over the inheritance. Mahadev had renounced the world, but not the bitterness. It festered quietly in the corners of his devotion.

Guruji took him for a walk to the hill behind the Ashram. There, he asked him to **carry a heavy stone** tied in a cloth. For days, Mahadev carried it—during meditations, meals, even walks.

"What is this stone?" Guruji finally asked.

Mahadev replied, *"It's the anger. It has become a part of me."*

Guruji said, *"No. It is what you're still holding. The stone has no will—only you do."*

Mahadev finally untied the cloth and left the stone at the hilltop. That moment wasn't dramatic—but over time, his chanting changed. His eyes softened. His joy returned.

"The learning?" Apeksha said, "Even monks can carry silent prisons. Forgiveness isn't weakness—it is permission to stop bleeding for wounds others gave."

The circle sat in silence, eyes moist, some with closed lids—not asleep, but absorbing. Stories like these weren't mere narratives. They were **mirrors**. They held fragments of everyone's journey.

The afternoon light had shifted; shadows lengthened.

Kiran, leaning against the low trunk of the Banyan tree, let out a soft sigh—not impatient, but gently urging:

"Time for the next session…"

The devotees slowly rose, their bodies light, their hearts even lighter.

As they walked back toward Shambav Hall, Apeksha stayed back a moment, gazing up at the hanging roots above—like the memories of the cosmos, always reaching downward, waiting to be touched.

# CHAPTER VIII

## The Eternal Dance

*"Karma and manifestation are two rhythms of the same cosmic song—one remembers, the other creates."*

– Shree Shambav


### Synopsis

**Karma is the blueprint of your past; manifestation is the brush of your future.**

*The laws of cause and effect and the art of conscious creation are not separate paths—they are threads of the same divine tapestry. Karma does not arrive to punish, nor does manifestation exist to grant fleeting desires. Both are sacred, neutral forces—mirrors reflecting your deepest intentions and actions.*

*When you begin to see karma not as destiny carved in stone but as energy shaped by awareness, you unlock the power to rewrite your patterns. And when manifestation is no longer an act of wishful thinking, but a conscious alignment with your highest truth, life becomes not something that happens to you, but something that flows from you.*

*In this sacred dance between what has been and what can be, every moment becomes a brushstroke. With presence and purpose, you can turn cycles of pain into pathways of growth—sowing seeds not just for a better life, but for a more awakened one.*

## Manifestation and Karma—The Eternal Dance

As the golden rays of the afternoon sun filtered gently through the carved wooden lattices of Shambav Hall, a hushed stillness wrapped the room—not of silence, but of sacred anticipation.

After a long pause, Roopa spoke—her voice tender, but laced with a yearning that came from somewhere deep.

*"Guruji,"* she asked, *"how do past karmic imprints influence what we are capable of manifesting in our present life?"*

"Roopa," Guruji began, "imagine your soul as a long scroll—one not made of paper, but of light and memory. Each thought, action, and intention, from every lifetime you've lived, leaves a mark on this scroll. Some marks are like golden calligraphy—born of love, courage, compassion. Others are ink stains—fear, resentment, guilt—still wet, still smudging the words you try to write now."

Guruji paused. "Karma is not punishment," he said gently, "it is a pattern. Not a prison, but an imprint. It is the echo of yesterday vibrating in today's choices."

He motioned softly with his hand. "You may dream of manifesting love, abundance, peace—but if old imprints within you still whisper 'I am not worthy,' 'I must suffer to be seen,' or 'joy is unsafe'—then even the brightest desire may never take root."

Guruji, after a pause, said, "There was a seeker once—her name was Asha. She came here, much like you all, carrying a burning desire to live her purpose. She was a gifted healer, but every time she tried to share her gifts with the world, she was met with rejection or invisibility. Nothing seemed to move."

"One afternoon, in stillness, Asha was guided into deep karmic reflection. In her visions, she saw a mirror—ancient, cracked, and splintered. And within its fragments, past lifetimes emerged: one where she was betrayed for speaking truth, another where her healing was condemned as heresy. In each lifetime, she learned to silence herself—not out of weakness, but survival."

Guruji looked around the room, his voice softer now. "Those karmic shards were still embedded in her energetic body. Though she desired visibility, her soul remembered danger. Though she wanted to manifest light, her subconscious feared the dark that had followed her light before."

"But here's the miracle," he smiled, "awareness is the alchemy."

Through meditation, guidance, and presence, Asha began to reclaim those parts—not to erase them, but to honour them. And with that honouring, the ink stains began to dissolve. Her scroll became writable again. And soon, effortlessly, her gifts reached those who needed them—not through striving, but through alignment."

### The River and the Stones

"Imagine a river that wants to reach the ocean," Guruji continued. "Manifestation is that river's flow. But karma—unprocessed and unconscious—are the stones lying beneath.

The river cannot flow freely until those stones are seen, understood, and, in some cases, removed or redirected."

"But those same stones can be used," he added, "to build bridges, once you know they're there."

"So you see, Roopa," Guruji concluded with warmth, "it is not that karma blocks your manifestation—it is that karma reveals where love must still flow. The universe does not withhold your desires; it waits for you to become whole enough to receive them."

Guruji rested his hand on his chest, closing his eyes: **"When we bring light to the imprints we carry—with compassion, not judgment—judgment-the future no longer repeats the past. It transforms it."**

A long silence followed—but it wasn't empty. It was filled with the quiet awe of recognition.

And in that moment, many hearts silently vowed:

*To no longer fear the past,*

*But to read it,*

*Reclaim it,*

*And rise from it.*


As the shadows lengthened across the red stone floors of Shambav Hall. Some birds sang softly outside, their melodies weaving into the stillness as if nature itself were eavesdropping.

Guruji sat with his eyes gently closed, his breathing deep and even—not asleep, but in some unspoken communion.

Then, Akshaya leaned forward—his voice clear, steady, but edged with an ache he didn't mask.

*"Guruji," he asked, "in what ways can conscious manifestation act as a tool for resolving or transcending karmic patterns?"*

Guruji simply held the silence between the question and its unfolding, as if letting the inquiry stretch into the ether.

**The Seed and the Flame**

"Akshaya," he said softly, "Karma is like a seed buried deep within the soil of your being. It carries within it the memory of what you once planted—knowingly or unknowingly. Some of these seeds grow into flowers of wisdom. Others into thorns of repetition."

"Conscious manifestation is like a flame—not one that burns the seed blindly, but one that brings light into the soil itself."

He paused, his voice rich with meaning.

"To manifest consciously is to choose—not just what you want, but why you want it, and who you are becoming in the process. When you do this, you don't just manifest things—you manifest liberation."

Guurji, after a pause said, "Suren was a wanderer of many lifetimes—a brilliant mind, sharp and charismatic. But again and again, in every venture, he met betrayal. In business, in friendship, even in love—the pattern chased him like a shadow."

"Suren came not to ask why it kept happening, but how to break it. That was his power—his readiness."

Together, uncovered lifetimes where Suren had made decisions from fear—manipulating outcomes, seeking control, building walls instead of trust. The betrayals he experienced were not punishments—they were echoes. Echoes of the distrust he had sown before. Echoes of a soul that wanted to learn trust by tasting its absence.

"So I asked him," Guruji said gently, "What do you truly wish to manifest?"

"Suren said, 'Authentic relationships. Where I don't have to hide.'"

"And so I told him: Good. Then become the one who doesn't hide—not even from your pain."

Suren began a conscious journey—not of demanding loyalty from others, but of offering transparency from within. Each relationship became a mirror. Each challenge, an invitation to stay open instead of being armoured.

"And the karmic pattern," Guruji said, "did not 'end' overnight. But it began to change form. Instead of loops, his life became a spiral—returning, yes, but always higher."

**The Wound as the Portal**

"Karmic patterns," Guruji said, "are not chains. They are invitations. They are the soul's way of saying: **Here. Look again. Heal here.**"

"To manifest consciously is to look at your deepest longings not as cravings, but as compass needles. Why do you long for abundance? Perhaps because a past version of you once lived in scarcity and forgot what it meant to be held by life. Why do you long for freedom? Maybe because your soul remembers lifetimes of silence and shackles."

"But here is the shift," he said, his voice gentle but fierce:

"When your desire becomes not an escape from pain, but a prayer for wholeness—you transcend the karma that once defined you."

**The Mirror and the Window**

"Conscious manifestation," he added, "is both a mirror and a window. It shows you what still lives within. And it opens into what is waiting to be born."

He looked around the hall—many eyes were moist now, not from sorrow, but from recognition. Something unsaid had become undeniable.

*"You are not bound by your past," Guruji said finally. "But you are guided by it—if you're willing to see it as a teacher instead of a curse."*

And then, in a tone soft like dusk, Guruji offered the closing thread:

*"Every conscious act of creation is an act of redemption.*

*Each time you choose love over fear, truth over pretence, courage over habit —*

*you not only create a new reality —*

*you release an old one."*

And the hall fell silent once more—not empty, but full of the seeds that had just been lit by fire.

As Guruji's words settled like sacred ash across the hearts of those gathered, the air in Shambav Hall grew thick with silence—not of absence, but of presence. Outside, the rustling leaves whispered against the ancient stone walls. Inside, each listener sat still, as if the breath of time had paused to listen too.

It was Nita who finally broke the silence—not with words at first, but with a slow, steady breath, as though exhaling lifetimes of burden she didn't know she'd been holding.

She turned slightly, her gaze seeking Kiran, whose eyes were already damp—wide open, yet looking inward, as if the past had knocked gently and he had dared to answer.

Nita spoke softly, but clearly.

*"Guruji's words..."* she said, almost to herself, *"they remind me of something I've often felt but never fully understood—that maybe what we think of as suffering... is not punishment, but a delayed prayer being answered through refinement."*

She paused, eyes shimmering.

"When Guruji spoke of Suren," she continued, "I saw my own reflection. I've always longed for belonging—in family, in love, even in work. And every time I thought I'd found it, life would pull it away."

"I used to think it meant I wasn't meant to have it. But now…" she looked up, as if seeing the ceiling for the first time, "I wonder if I was being asked to become—to become the belonging I kept seeking."

The hall remained hushed, yet something stirred in everyone—a quiet tremor of truth, recognised and respected.

Kiran, his voice low and almost reverent, added:

*"I always thought karma was some cosmic accountant keeping score. But today… I saw it differently. Maybe karma is not about being punished for what you did… maybe it's about being reminded of what you forgot."*

He looked down at his hands.

*"I forgot my own power. I've lived reacting, not creating. Blaming fate instead of listening to it."*

He turned to Akshaya with a soft smile.

"Your question, Akshaya… it opened something. Conscious manifestation isn't just about dreaming big—it's about remembering who we are beneath the noise of who we've been told to be."

Guruji's eyes gently met theirs—no need for more words.

Outside, the wind moved through the banyan leaves as though offering its own applause—not loud, but eternal.

*Padma asked, "Guruji, can the act of setting new intentions realign our karmic path—and if so, how does awareness shift the outcome of our manifestations?"*

The Shambav Hall was silent again—that sacred kind of silence which comes not from the absence of sound, but from the deep stillness that arrives when a question touches the soul of everyone present.

Padma's voice had carried something more than words—it carried a longing. A longing not to escape karma, but to dance with it more wisely. Guruji looked at her with the softness of a moonlit lake.

He took a sip of warm water from the copper vessel beside him and gently began.

**The Weaver's Loom**

"Padma," Guruji said, "Imagine your life as a tapestry—woven thread by thread. Each thread represents a thought, a choice, a moment. The karmic patterns are like designs stitched from the past—some beautiful, some tangled. And yes, many were sewn unconsciously."

"But the loom," Guruji paused, "the loom is always in your hands."

He let the silence hold that thought before continuing.

"Setting a new intention is like choosing a new thread. It doesn't erase the old design, but it begins to reweave the fabric. When the act of intention is conscious, it becomes sacred. It realigns the tapestry, not just at the edge where you begin again, but through the whole pattern—because intention, when rooted in awareness, changes the *weaver*, not just the *weaving*."

Guruji's eyes softened as he leaned back slightly, hands folded in his lap. "There was once a woman named Kamalini, who came to the ashram many years ago. She had spent most of her life serving others—a dutiful daughter, devoted wife, mother of three. But in her silence, she was bitter. She felt invisible. Used."

"She came to me not asking for peace, but for permission—to leave it all, run away and start over. She said, *'Guruji, I've given everything. Now I want something for myself. Is it wrong?'*"

"I asked her, *What is it that you truly seek—revenge on your past, or a reconciliation with your own soul?*"

"She cried," Guruji whispered. "Not because she didn't know the answer. But because for the first time, she allowed herself to hear it."

"So we sat. We meditated. And from her heart rose a new intention—not to escape her life, but to live it with presence. Her karma wasn't her prison—her unconsciousness was."

"She began small," Guruji smiled, "taking ten minutes every morning just to sit by herself under a neem tree. That silence became her sanctuary. Slowly, she changed her words. She chose love over resentment, not because others deserved it—but because *she* did."

"And over time, her home changed. Not because others transformed first. But because her *intention* changed, her vibration. And her vibration rewrote the energy of her karma."

## The Compass and the Map

"Padma," Guruji continued, "Karma is like a map—it tells you where you've been, what roads have worn you, where patterns have repeated."

"But *intention* is your compass. It cannot erase the terrain, but it can change the direction."

"When you set an intention—with clarity, with love, with surrender—you invite awareness to walk beside you. And awareness is what separates fate from freedom."

He gestured toward the small flame flickering at the front of the hall.

"Without awareness, fire burns. With awareness, it cooks your food, lights your path, warms your soul."

Guruji closed his eyes briefly and then opened them again, his gaze resting on everyone—but somehow looking deeper, as if he was seeing them not just in this life, but across lifetimes.

*"You are not here to undo the past. You are here to rewrite your relationship with it. Every new intention, held in awareness, becomes a lightpost along the path—not to escape your karma, but to transcend its unconscious repetition."*

"And that," Guruji said softly, "is the beginning of liberation."

The afternoon sun had mellowed into a golden hue, casting dappled patterns through the carved windows of the Shambav Hall. Outside, the Banyan leaves whispered softly in the wind. Inside, stillness held the air like sacred breath—that pregnant hush after deep contemplation.

Vasudeva leaned slightly forward, his palms open in quiet inquiry.

*"Guruji,"* he asked, his voice measured but stirred by inner weight, *"What is the difference between karmic manifestations driven by unconscious habits, and manifestations created through mindful, deliberate choices?"*

There was a long pause.

Guruji smiled—not out of amusement, but as if acknowledging the depth of the question. He closed his eyes for a brief moment, as though listening to something more ancient than thought itself.

**The Two Gardens**

"Vasudeva," he began, "imagine two gardens."

"One is wild, left untended. Seeds have been sown, not by intent, but by repetition—the same weeds, the same thorns. They return season after season because no one notices them sprouting. That is the garden of *unconscious karma*. It does not ask for your permission. It grows by momentum."

"The other garden," he continued, "is cared for with awareness. Each seed is chosen, planted with love. The gardener knows that every flower begins as an intention. That is the garden of *conscious manifestation.*"

He looked at Vasudeva gently.

"The difference is not in the soil. It is in the awareness of the sower."

"Let me tell you about Rehan," Guruji said.

"He was a man with a good heart, but a restless soul. He kept changing careers, relationships, even homes—always searching, always leaving. He would say, *'I just follow where life takes me.'* It sounded poetic, but it was not freedom. It was avoidance."

"One day, after his third divorce and the failure of another business, he sat here, where you sit now, and asked me, *'Why does this keep happening to me? Am I cursed?'*"

"I told him, *Rehan, you are not cursed. You are consistent. You are loyal to your unconscious patterns. That is all.*"

Guruji continued, "We traced his karmic pattern. Not through regression, but through reflection. Rehan realised that he had carried a fear of stability from childhood—his father left, his home was unsafe, and in every lifetime since, he mistook *chaos* for *freedom*. He kept manifesting the same endings… because he never questioned the beginning."

Guruji said, "A simple practice was given. *Do nothing impulsively for 21 days. Observe. Choose slowly.*"

"Those 21 days became his turning point. It wasn't easy. He cried. He wanted to run. But for the first time, he stayed—

with himself. That pause birthed awareness. And from that awareness, he set a new intention: *to create, not escape.*"

"Today, he's a counselor—guiding others through the storms he once drowned in. His past didn't change. But his relationship with it did."

Guruji turned his palm upward.

"Karmic manifestations from the unconscious are like looking into a mirror without realising it's a reflection. We react. We blame. We repeat. The mirror doesn't lie—but it also doesn't create."

"But when you become a sculptor—aware, patient, intentional—you don't just reflect. You shape. You transform. You chisel a new form from the same stone."

"The universe is neutral," Guruji added softly. "It responds not to your words, but to your vibration. And your vibration is shaped by your *state of consciousness.*"

## The Invitation

"Vasudeva," Guruji said, "your question is not just philosophical. It is practical. Every moment is a fork: will you water the weeds or tend the seeds?"

"The unconscious karmic path is like a river flowing downhill—predictable, habitual, effortless, but often unconscious. Conscious manifestation is like learning to swim upstream—slow at first, tiring, but eventually… it gives you choice. And from choice, comes *grace.*"

He placed his hand on his heart.

"You are not here to fight your karma. You are here to wake up within it."

As the golden hue of the sun stretched its final light across the horizon, Guruji, after a long contemplative pause, gently folded his palms and said, "Let us take a brief pause before we gather again."

The devotees slowly rose, their hearts still steeped in the depth of the afternoon's discourse.

Akshaya, Sam, Nita, Lalitha, and many others made their way toward the ancient Banyan tree, whose wide branches cradled the sky like a sage in silent meditation. Beneath its canopy, a gentle gathering took form—a moment suspended in time.

Kiran and a few others, with simple grace, served steaming cups of herbal tea. The fragrance of tulsi, lemongrass, and cardamom wove through the air like an offering. The devotees cradled their cups as if holding warmth itself, both in hands and heart.

They sat in loose circles on the cool earth, their discussions soft and reverent, their words meandering through themes of karma, memory, and the mystery of manifestation. The air had shifted—the sun was retreating slowly, brushing the clouds in saffron and rose. A cool breeze began to stir, carrying with it the humming tones of wind through the leaves, like nature's own mantra echoing through the sacred grove.

Birds began to nestle into quietude, their songs winding down to a hush, while the first stars timidly revealed themselves—

tiny pinholes of light in the indigo sky, watching silently over the gathering.

Then—a soft chime, distant but clear, drifted from the Shambav Hall, the bell of return.

Like a gentle call from the Infinite, it stirred something within them—not urgency, but devotion. One by one, Akshaya and the others stood, their eyes still reflecting the stillness of the dusk. With calm anticipation, they began making their way back toward the Hall—their steps slow, like a silent procession returning to a temple not just of stone, but of soul.

The evening session was about to begin. And within each heart, something quiet had already awakened.

# CHAPTER IX

## The Heart's Role in Manifestation

*"Emotion is the silent architect that gives form to thought—without its rhythm, even the clearest intention remains unbuilt."*

– Shree Shambav

### Synopsis

**Manifestation is not merely a mental exercise—it is an emotional alchemy.**

*Thoughts may set direction, but feelings provide momentum. Emotions are the magnetic undercurrents that draw reality toward you, amplifying intentions into form. The subtle yet profound harmony between heart and mind—known as heart-brain coherence—becomes the fertile ground where true manifestation takes root.*

*Emotional intelligence is not just awareness of feelings, but the wisdom to navigate them, transform them, and align them with purpose. When your inner state resonates with clarity, compassion, and conviction, your outer world begins to echo that resonance.*

*Manifestation becomes less about chasing outcomes and more about becoming the frequency of what you desire. In this space of inner harmony, the universe responds—not with randomness, but with precision. You do not force reality; you flow with it. You do not demand; you align. And what is aligned never delays.*

## Emotional Intelligence—The Heart's Role in Manifestation

As the soft twilight spilled its golden hue into the Shambav Hall, the devotees sat in reverent stillness. The wind hummed through the open windows, rustling the edges of saffron robes and prayer scarves. A lamp flickered near Guruji's seat—steady, luminous.

Vidyarthi's voice rose with a quiet fire: "Guruji, how does emotional intelligence influence the frequency and clarity of our manifestations?"

Guruji smiled, gently nodding before it was even spoken.

The Mirror Lake and the Storm

"Vidyarthi," Guruji began, his voice calm like the hush before rainfall,

"Imagine two lakes."

"One is agitated—a storm has swept through. Winds churn the waters, and the surface is wild with movement. Drop a seed in it, and it vanishes. No reflection forms. No clarity remains. This is the emotional state of most people: they desire to manifest, but their inner waters are chaotic—stirred by unhealed wounds, fears, suppressed anger, or craving without awareness."

He paused, letting the image settle.

"Now imagine another lake—serene, still, reflective. When a single seed drops in, *ripples form with grace*. The seed can take root. The sky mirrors back. This lake is the heart governed by emotional intelligence—where awareness has met emotion, and turned it into insight."

"There was once a young artist named Meera," Guruji continued, "gifted, but unknown. She painted not for galleries, but for survival. Her work was skilful but hollow. She painted what others demanded—pretty things, safe subjects. She lived from fear—fear of rejection, of not being enough, of losing the little she had."

"One day, after a personal loss, she broke. Her emotions overflowed—grief, rage, loneliness. But instead of escaping them, she entered them. A mentor guided her gently to *feel*, not *flee*. To listen, not label."

"Through that pain, she awakened something new—a voice in her art that had long been buried. She painted from truth. Her grief became brushstrokes, her longing became colour. She was no longer just creating art—she was transmitting frequency. Her pain became sacred, her joy authentic. And with that, her paintings began to attract not just buyers, but seekers. People said: *I see myself in her work*. She became successful not because she tried to manifest it, but because she aligned emotionally with her essence."

## Emotion as the Tuning Fork

"Emotional intelligence," Guruji said, turning slightly toward Vidyarthi, "is not about controlling your emotions. It is about *communing* with them. Listening to anger and learning where your boundary was broken. Sitting with sadness and discovering where love was lost."

"When you bring conscious awareness to your emotional currents, you stop manifesting by accident. Your intentions gain clarity. You begin to transmit with a frequency that matches not just desire—but *truth*."

He placed his hand on his heart.

"When heart and mind beat in coherence, your energy becomes undeniable—and what is meant for you will not need to be chased. It will recognise you."

## The Garden Within

"Emotions," Guruji said, "are like the soil of manifestation. If filled with stones of resentment, weeds of fear, and dryness of doubt, even the most powerful seed—your intention—cannot grow."

"But if the soil is nourished with understanding, compassion, self-awareness… your life becomes a garden. And the universe, like the sun, can finally find you."

*Aastha, her voice was soft, yet filled with sincerity "Guruji, in what ways can heart-brain coherence strengthen our connection with the energy field of manifestation?"*

Guruji turned slowly, as though tuning in not just to her words but to the silence beneath them. A smile touched his face—calm, kind, and luminous.

## The Drum and the Dancer

"Dear Aastha," Guruji began, "imagine a tribal dancer circling a fire at night. The body follows the beat of the drum, and the drum follows the rhythm of the heart. If the dancer moves without listening to the drum, the dance becomes chaotic. If the drummer beats without attuning to the dancer, the fire of movement fades. But when both are in sync—body and beat, will and rhythm—a sacred trance begins. The energy becomes palpable, and the circle becomes a portal."

He paused. "In the same way, the heart and brain are like the dancer and the drum. When they are in harmony—when the emotional pulse of the heart and the cognitive clarity of the mind move as one—you enter the sacred rhythm of creation itself."

## The Forgotten Healer

Guruji said, "There was once a woman named Sharvani who came here years ago," he said. "On the surface, she was accomplished—a doctor, a mother, a leader. But beneath it all, she felt disconnected. Her mind was sharp, but her heart was weary. She manifested achievements, yes, but not joy. Not peace."

Guruji sipped from his copper tumbler and continued.

"Through deep inner work and guided meditation, we helped her return to her heart. She wept—not for pain, but for having forgotten its language. She began practices to align breath, feeling, and thought—heart-brain coherence."

Guruji drew a slow, deep breath, inviting everyone to do the same.

"She discovered that when she set intentions from that coherent state—not from anxiety, but from deep love and clarity—her life began to respond differently. Patients who once resisted healing began to improve. Her children opened up to her in new ways. Opportunities aligned with ease, not struggle. It was as though the universe had been waiting for her to tune her inner instrument before playing its melody."

**The Unified Field Responds to Harmony**

"The energy field of manifestation," Guruji continued, "is not unlike a mirror. But it does not reflect just your thoughts—it reflects your total vibration. The heart generates the largest electromagnetic field in the body. When it beats in rhythm with your higher emotions—compassion, gratitude, courage—it becomes a signal the universe cannot ignore. Add to that the focused clarity of the brain, and you become like a finely tuned instrument—transmitting intention with resonance."

Guruji smiled softly at Aastha.

"You asked how heart-brain coherence strengthens our connection to manifestation. The answer is: it transforms you from a scattered signal into a resonant frequency. And that frequency doesn't attract just outcomes—it attracts alignment. It attracts meaning. It attracts wholeness."

## The Still Flame Within

Gurujiu placed his hand gently on his chest.

"Manifestation is not just about having what you want—it is about becoming who you truly are. When the heart and mind unite, you stop pushing life, and life begins to flow through you. In that space, manifestation is no longer effortful. It becomes inevitable."

A hush followed, not out of quiet but out of reverence. The room seemed to exhale in unison, a field of hearts remembering their rhythm.

As the evening deepened, a hush fell upon the Shambav Hall. The warm glow of the oil lamps danced on the walls like ancient memories revisiting the present. The devotees sat in stillness—not out of discipline, but devotion. A kind of sacred anticipation hung in the air, like the pause before the first monsoon raindrop touches parched earth.

*Abhirami, draped in a soft indigo shawl, gently leaned forward and asked with a voice ripe with longing, "Guruji, how do unresolved emotions sabotage or distort the manifestation process, even when thoughts are clear?"*

Guruji looked at her with tender eyes—not the gaze of a teacher dispensing knowledge, but of a sage who had wandered through storms and understood the language of silent suffering.

## The Still Surface and the Hidden Currents

"Abhirami," Guruji began softly, "imagine a lake. On the surface, the water is still, reflecting the moon with perfect clarity. This is your mind—focused, calm, filled with clear intentions. But beneath the surface, if there are restless currents—unresolved emotions, suppressed fears, old griefs—they ripple upward. Though the moon above is whole, its reflection shimmers and distorts."

He paused. "You may believe your thoughts are aligned. But if your emotions—the deeper water—carry doubt, resentment, guilt, or sorrow, the signal you send out to the universe is not of clarity, but contradiction."

## The Lantern and the Smoke

"To manifest is to light a lantern," he continued. "Your thought is the flame, but your emotion is the oil. If the oil is clean—love, trust, gratitude—the flame burns bright and steady. But if the oil is tainted—with bitterness, unhealed wounds, or repressed shame—the lantern smokes. The light flickers. And the path ahead is clouded."

He turned slightly, gesturing toward the back of the hall, as though conjuring a memory from the space itself.

Guruji after a pause said, "There was once a young woman named Sneha who came here. Intelligent, focused, deeply spiritual. She wrote daily affirmations, meditated diligently, visualised a harmonious marriage, meaningful work, and a life of service. Her mind was a sharp arrow—but life kept circling back with disappointments. Relationships would bloom and then wither. Work opportunities would come close but slip away. She was frustrated and confused. 'I'm doing everything right,' she said. 'Why does nothing manifest fully?'"

Guruji looked into the flickering flame of a nearby lamp and said gently, "I asked her, 'What have you not forgiven?'"

She was silent.

Then slowly, painfully, she opened up—about a letter she never sent. A letter she had written to her father who abandoned their family. A letter filled with pain, but also truth—a truth she never voiced aloud. She had buried the emotion beneath years of spiritual practice, mistaking avoidance for peace.

"When Sneha finally read the letter aloud—not to send it, but to set it free—she wept. The emotion she had locked away began to flow. And for the first time, her thoughts and her emotions met—like the river finally rejoining the ocean."

Within months, her life shifted. Not because of magic—but because the contradiction within her signal dissolved. The heart no longer denied what the mind claimed to want. The oil burned clean.

**The Frequency of Truth**

"Unresolved emotions," Guruji continued, "carry a vibration of their own. They whisper into the field of creation, whether you acknowledge them or not. The universe does not respond to your polished words—it responds to your whole vibration."

He let the silence settle.

"To manifest is not to paste joy over grief. It is to meet the grief with love, to hold the shame with compassion, to allow the tears to fall not as signs of weakness, but as baptisms of truth."

He turned to Abhirami and added with a gentleness that cracked open hearts:

"You asked how unresolved emotions distort manifestation. They do not stop it—they redirect it. They create a reality not of your mind's clarity, but of your soul's hidden chaos. The key is not control—it is congruence. The inner must match the outer."

## The Alchemy of Healing

"Do not be afraid to feel," Guruji whispered. "Your emotions are not interruptions on the path. They *are* the path. When you allow them, they become allies. When you resist them, they become shadows."

A bird rustled in the ancient banyan outside. The wind sighed through the open arches. The room felt heavier—not in burden, but in sacred presence.

The devotees sat unmoving, eyes wide not with wonder, but remembrance.

Abhirami folded her hands, her eyes moist. No more questions arose. The answer had touched something deeper than words.

*Kiran's voice rose—steady yet yearning.* "Guruji," *he asked,* "what practices can help us consciously cultivate emotions that align with our desires, rather than with our doubts or fears?"

Guruji's eyes softened. A smile played on his lips—the kind that blooms from compassion forged through lifetimes of listening.

## The Instrument and the Tuning

"Kiran," Guruji said, "emotions are not random guests; they are musicians in the orchestra of your inner life. Your desires are like the melody you wish to play—joy, peace, abundance, love. But if your emotional instruments are out of tune—if fear plays a louder note than faith, or doubt drowns the rhythm of hope—then even the right melody will sound discordant."

He looked at the gathering, each soul with silent symphonies waiting to be heard.

"To align your emotions with your desires is not to force the song—it is to tune the instruments."

Guruji leaned slightly, as though drawing a memory from the fabric of space.

"There was a man named Kapil," Guruji began. "He wanted to manifest a new life—a career with meaning, a relationship with depth, a home where he could breathe peace. He read every book on manifestation, practised affirmations, and visualised every day. But nothing changed."

Guruji paused. "So I asked him, 'Tell me, what do you feel most often?' He replied, 'Anxiety. And sometimes, an undercurrent of unworthiness.'"

Guruji's gaze grew deeper, like a well of insight. "I told him, 'You are trying to paint a new picture on a wall soaked with old water. Until you drain the room of what was—the dampness of fear, the mould of shame—no colour will last. You don't need more paint. You need sunlight.'"

So Kapil began a different practice—not of seeking more, but of tending to what was already within. He started each morning with breathwork and silence—not to escape anxiety, but to greet it. He wrote letters to the version of himself that felt unworthy—not to judge him, but to love him.

Slowly, the emotional waters cleared.

And then, without striving—doors opened. Not because he shouted his desires to the universe, but because he became a match to them.

**Tending the Garden of Emotion**

Guruji turned back to Kiran. "You asked what practices help us align emotions with our desires? Let me offer you a few—not as prescriptions, but as invitations."

1. Emotional Rehearsal with Presence

"Every morning," he said, "before you rise into the noise of the world, sit with your heart. Not with your checklist—but with your desired feeling. If you long for joy, remember a moment of joy, and breathe into it. Rehearse it not as an actor fakes a smile, but as a gardener waters the roots."

2. The Mirror Ritual

"Stand before a mirror. Look not just at your reflection—but into your eyes. Speak to your fears as you would to a child. Tell them they are seen. That they no longer have to drive. Then speak your desires aloud, gently, firmly—as a promise to your soul."

3. Gratitude as Frequency Stabiliser

"Gratitude," he said, "is the most stable emotional frequency. It is the only feeling that says 'yes' to life even when life says 'wait.' Keep a daily list—but more than the list, feel the warmth each entry brings. Gratitude trains your emotions to rest in abundance, not in lack."

4. Breath and Body Alignment

"The body stores the emotions the mind has forgotten. Practice breathwork—not to silence emotion, but to let it flow. Movement, dance, even silent walking… these are ways to tell your emotional body: 'You are safe to feel again.'"

5. Emotional Contrast Journaling

"Each time you feel doubt," Guruji continued, "write it down. Then on the opposite page, write what the highest version of you would say instead. This is not denial—it is rewiring."

**When the Soil is Ready**

Guruji closed his eyes for a moment. Then, softly, "A seed doesn't need to beg the earth to grow. It only needs the right soil. Emotion is that soil. Align your feelings with the truth of your desire—not the echo of your past—and manifestation becomes not a struggle, but a flowering."

Guruji turned to Kiran, who sat still, a tear quietly tracing the path of truth down his cheek.

"Manifestation," Guruji whispered, "is not about demanding from the universe. It's about becoming what the universe already wants to give you. But the universe will not violate your frequency—it will wait, patiently, until you are ready to receive in the same energy you seek."

Guruji, after a long pause, slowly rose from his asana. He folded his hands in Atma Namaste, his eyes soft, as if holding a universe within. Without a word, he stepped away from the Shambav Hall. The day's session had ended, but the silence he left behind lingered—like the echo of a temple bell that vibrates in the chest long after it is heard.

One by one, the devotees rose from their seats, still wrapped in the depth of the discourse. Outside the hall, the night had wrapped the land in its quiet beauty. A cool breeze brushed against their faces. The sky was a canopy of stars—countless, calm, and comforting. Fireflies danced softly among the trees, as if the stars themselves had descended to witness the earth.

Vasudeva and Padma, sensing the need for reflection, gently called out to the others, "Let's gather near the fireplace after dinner." The rest nodded silently, still soaking in the atmosphere.

Later, with the meal complete, the group slowly gathered around the fire. Akshaya, Alice, Sofia, Bhavya, Aarna, Dev, and others joined, some sitting on logs, others on folded mats. The fire crackled, throwing golden sparks into the night. They began discussing the day's revelations—manifestation, emotions, karmic blueprints—each sharing their reflections in soft, contemplative tones.

Martina, breaking the flow of conversation with her bright curiosity, turned to Apeksha and said, "Why don't you share a story? Something from the past… maybe a moment from the ashram or retreat. Your stories… they stay with us."

Before Apeksha could respond, Padma smiled and raised her hand gently. "I remember two stories," she said, her voice carrying the weight of remembrance. The firelight flickered on her face, giving her an almost ethereal glow. "Both changed how I saw manifestation. Both showed me how Guruji doesn't just teach—he transforms."

## The First Story: The Mirror Within

"There was a woman who came to the ashram named Revathi," Padma began. "She was vibrant, articulate, and yet… always searching. She had a vision board full of dreams—she wanted success, a partner, peace, recognition. She was doing everything: affirmations, rituals, visualisations. But nothing… nothing seemed to manifest."

"One evening, during darshan, Guruji simply asked her, 'When you look in the mirror, who do you see?' Revathi said, 'I see someone who is trying her best.'"

"Guruji looked at her gently and said, 'Trying is a bridge, but what do you truly *believe*? Not just in thought, but in feeling?' Revathi was silent. And then she wept—not because she didn't know, but because she did. Deep down, she believed she wasn't worthy of the very dreams she was chasing."

"She stayed for weeks after that, not to learn how to manifest, but to *feel worthy* of manifesting. Guruji taught her to hold herself like she would hold her own child. To sit in the morning sun and say, 'I am already whole.'"

"And slowly, things shifted—not because the world changed first, but because she did. The partner came. The work blossomed. But more than anything, she stopped chasing light... because she realised she *was* the light."

**Ashes and Seeds**

Padma's gaze turned inward, softer now. "The second story is about a young man named Tejas. He came to the retreat after losing his father. He had just begun building his life, and it all crumbled. He was angry—with the world, with fate, and most of all... with God."

"He didn't believe in manifestation. He said, 'What's the point? Everything I love is taken.' Guruji didn't offer platitudes. He simply asked Tejas to take care of a dying jasmine plant outside his hut."

"It was winter. The plant looked barren. For weeks, Tejas watered it, pruned its branches, sat by it in silence—sometimes crying, sometimes raging. And then… one morning, a single flower bloomed."

"He came running to Guruji, holding that fragile blossom. 'It lived!' he said. Guruji smiled and replied, 'And so did you.'"

"Tejas realised that manifestation isn't always about acquiring—it's often about *restoring* our faith, our spirit, our will to live beautifully. That jasmine wasn't just a flower. It was a mirror of his own rebirth."

Padma's voice trailed into silence. The fire crackled, and the wind hummed gently through the trees. The night was long, the stars were listening, and even the fireflies seemed to pause in reverence.

No one spoke for a while. It was the kind of silence that didn't ask to be filled.

Then, from the shadows, Kiran exhaled deeply. "Let's rest," he said softly. "Tomorrow… another sunrise. Another step."

And just like that, the gathering disbanded. Some left with tears in their eyes, others with quiet smiles. But all walked away with something invisible, something sacred—like seeds newly planted in the garden of their souls.

# PART THREE

## Manifestation in Action

*"Daily practices are not routines—they are sacred conversations between who you are and who you are becoming."*

- Shree Shambav

# CHAPTER X

## How to Manifest Consciously

*"A dream confined to thought is a bird with clipped wings, but when aligned action meets intention, even the impossible takes flight."*

– Shree Shambav

### Synopsis

*A practical awakening unfolds here, guiding you from unconscious patterns into the art of intentional creation. It reveals how to break free from limiting cycles and step fully into your power as a conscious manifestor. Through the integration of affirmations, visualisation, mindfulness, emotional mastery, and self-love, this journey helps you realign thought, feeling, and action into a living blueprint for the reality you truly desire. Conscious manifestation becomes more than a method—it transforms into a lifestyle rooted in clarity, purpose, and deep alignment with the universe.*

### Breaking Free—How to Manifest Consciously

The morning was pleasant—a soft golden light filtered through the tall windows of Shambav Hall, casting delicate patterns on the stone floor. Birds sang as if in prayer, and the gentle hum of anticipation filled the air. Disciples had already gathered, seated in quiet rows, the silence between them rich with reverence.

After a few moments, the wooden doors opened, and Guruji entered.

Every soul rose instinctively, not out of obligation, but out of deep love and respect. He moved with the grace of someone who had long since surrendered his ego—each step grounded in presence. With folded hands in Atma Namaskar, and a serene smile that felt like sunlight on the soul, Guruji acknowledged them all. He took his asana and sat in stillness.

Moments passed like petals falling from a timeless tree.

Then, breaking the silence yet not disturbing its sanctity, a seeker named Vidyarthi rose. His voice carried the weight of sincere inquiry.

*"Guruji," he asked, "are we living by design or by default? How often do our daily thoughts and actions reflect unconscious conditioning rather than intentional creation—and what small changes can we make today to break that cycle?"*

Guruji looked at Vidyarthi, his eyes reflecting the sky—boundless, accepting, unhurried.

He pointed gently toward the open window, where a quiet stream shimmered through the distant fields. "Do you see that stream?" he asked. "It flows not because it chooses to—but because its path was carved long ago. By roots. By rocks. By time itself. It surrenders to the shape given to it, unaware of its own ability to rise, evaporate, and return as rain—choosing a new place to fall."

He paused, letting the metaphor ripple into silence.

"In the same way, most human lives are lived by *default*. We wake as our parents woke. We speak the language of our childhood fears. We make decisions shaped by old wounds, unexamined beliefs, and inherited patterns. Our habits wear grooves in the mind, and we flow along them—unconscious, automatic."

Vidyarthi listened, his breath caught between understanding and awe.

"But," Guruji continued, "you are not the stream. You are the *sky*. Vast. Infinite. Capable of transformation at any moment. To live by *design* is to remember this truth."

Guruji leaned forward slightly, the light falling across his face like a blessing.

"Intentional creation is not a grand performance. It is born in small, sacred choices:

- **Awareness before reaction**—When emotion stirs, pause and ask, '*Is this truly me, or a story I've been told?*' That moment of stillness is where freedom begins.

- **Intention before action**—Even simple acts—drinking water, speaking a word, opening a door—can carry the power of consciousness when done with presence.

- **Compassion in correction**—When old patterns return, don't condemn yourself. Smile. You've caught the cycle. That's progress, not failure."

He looked across the hall, meeting each eye with unwavering love.

"To live by design is not to control life, but to co-create with it—in clarity, in courage, and in communion with the universe."

Outside, the wind stirred the leaves of the old Peepal tree. Inside, something even subtler stirred—a shift in perception, a silent promise to choose awareness over automation, design over default.

And in that still morning, in the heart of Shambav Hall, a new kind of day had already begun.

The morning light filtered gently into Shambav Hall, bathing the space in a soft glow that made everything feel timeless— as though even the air had memory. The sweet fragrance of sandalwood lingered, and the sounds of rustling leaves and distant temple bells wrapped the room in a meditative hush.

From the second row, a voice arose like a prayer carried on breath.

*It was Aastha. With folded hands and eyes brimming with sincerity, she asked, "Guruji, how do affirmations and visualisation bridge the gap between our inner world and outer reality? Why are mental rehearsals and emotionally charged affirmations more than mere words—and how do they act as seeds for future experiences?"*

Guruji slowly opened his eyes, the corners of his lips curving into a smile that felt like the first sunlight touching cold earth.

He didn't speak immediately. Instead, he pointed gently through the open window, toward the east garden, where a young sapling swayed lightly in the breeze.

"Do you see that sapling, Aastha?" he asked softly. "It bends now, unsure, finding its way to the sun. But buried within its roots lies the memory of a tree that has not yet come to be—tall, rooted, abundant with fruit and shelter. It doesn't just grow from the earth… it grows from a *blueprint* within."

He turned back to her, eyes now intense with truth. "Your thoughts—especially those spoken with emotion and clarity—are like that blueprint. An affirmation is not a wish; it is a code. A vibration. A sacred instruction whispered into the fabric of reality. And visualisation? That is the rehearsal of destiny. The mental act of aligning with what *already exists* in potential, but has not yet arrived in time."

The hall was still. Even the birds outside seemed to pause.

Guruji continued, "Most people rehearse pain far more faithfully than joy. Have you noticed? They imagine the worst before it happens. They replay wounds that were never fully theirs. That, too, is visualisation—unconscious, habitual, and self-fulfilling."

He paused for a moment, letting the weight of those words settle.

"But you can choose differently. When you speak an affirmation like, *'I am love. I am whole. I am open to miracles,'* you are not describing the present—you are invoking the truth beneath the noise. When you visualise your healing, your joy, your dharma unfolding—you are not being delusional; you are planting seeds in the unseen soil."

Guruji his voice rhythmic, "Imagine a sculptor standing before a raw block of stone. He does not *see* the stone. He sees the form within. Each affirmation is a chisel stroke. Each visualisation, a vision of the final form. The world only sees the dust—but he knows what he's freeing."

He leaned forward gently, meeting Aastha's eyes. "Speak to your soul as a gardener speaks to the earth. Not with doubt, but with devotion. Not with urgency, but with love. Let your affirmations be like morning light to a growing plant. Let your visualisations be the rain that feeds it. One day, that garden within will bloom into the life around you—and you will not call it magic. You will call it remembrance."

Aastha bowed slowly, her palms pressed to her heart. Something within her had shifted—not because she had learned something new, but because she had *remembered* something ancient.

The morning continued, but not as before. In the stillness of Shambav Hall, the unseen had been stirred—and new seeds, sown.

From among the seated seekers, Abhirami—her voice gentle but firm, like one who has walked through quiet storms.

*Abhirami bowed and asked, "Guruji, in what ways does self-love fuel authentic manifestation? Can we truly manifest abundance, love, and peace externally without cultivating them internally—and what does unconditional self-acceptance have to do with conscious creation?"*

A hush followed, deeper than silence. Some shifted slightly, others leaned in—not toward the sound, but toward the *presence* that would carry the response.

Guruji looked at Abhirami as one might look at a flower that had finally dared to bloom.

Guruji began softly, his voice steady, flowing like water over stone.

"Abhirami, you ask not just for yourself, but for every soul that has tried to build palaces on the sands of self-rejection."

He then turned his palm upward. "Tell me," he asked the room, "if this hand carries no warmth, can it give warmth to another? If the well is dry, how long can it quench another's thirst?"

The hall remained still, the question lingering in the air like a sacred bell that hadn't yet stopped ringing.

"You cannot manifest love if you have declared war against yourself," Guruji said. "You cannot create abundance from a heart anchored in unworthiness. Manifestation is not a trick of thought—it is the echo of your inner truth vibrating out into form."

Guruji then stood up—slowly, reverently—and walked a few steps to the open doorway. Outside, the garden lay vibrant in the sunlight.

"Come," he motioned. The disciples rose and quietly followed.

There in the garden stood two trees—one strong, with radiant green leaves and a quiet presence; the other smaller, with drooping branches and a visible struggle in its growth.

Guruji pointed. "This tree," he said, gesturing to the strong one, "receives everything it needs. Sunlight. Water. Nourishment. But most importantly, it accepts what it is. It does not compare its shape to the rose, nor envy the mango. It *thrives* because it doesn't resist its own nature."

Guruji turned to Abhirami. "You are like that tree. You were designed to flourish—not by changing into someone else, but by *loving what you are*. Self-love is not arrogance; it is alignment. It is knowing that you are not broken, but becoming."

A single leaf drifted to the earth as he continued.

"Every time you reject yourself—your scars, your mistakes, your softness—you create a split between what you desire and what you believe you deserve. That split becomes the very wall that blocks manifestation. But when you begin to accept yourself unconditionally—not as perfect, but as sacred—the wall dissolves. Your desires no longer echo against resistance… they flow into creation."

Guruji paused, then looked into her eyes with such presence that it seemed time stood still.

"Self-love is not indulgence—it is *grounding*. It tells the universe:
'I am ready to receive what is already mine.

'I am already whole, and now I call forth a life that reflects it.'"

He stepped back into the hall, and the seekers followed, something tender awakened in their hearts.

Settling once more into his asana, he closed with a story:

"There was once a potter who created a beautiful clay lamp—but he hid it in darkness, afraid it wasn't worthy to shine. It stayed hidden for years, until one day he lit a small flame inside. And suddenly, the lamp remembered why it had been made.

That flame, Abhirami… is self-love. The moment you light it, your life becomes the prayer it was always meant to be."

She bowed slowly, not just in gratitude—but in recognition.

And in that quiet moment, the light inside her flickered… and began to glow.

After Abhirami's heartfelt dialogue, a silence lingered—not empty, but pregnant with unseen truths.

*Then, from the front row, Kiran—a quiet seeker, slowly raised his hand. His voice was gentle, "Guruji," he asked, "How does mindful, aligned action transform thought into reality? Once intentions are set, why is aligned and inspired action a non-negotiable part of bringing our desires from the realm of thought into the world of form?"*

Guruji nodded slowly, as if Kiran had just placed a sacred key on the floor of the hall.

He sat back slightly, resting his hands on his knees, and closed his eyes for a moment before responding—not to think, but to feel. "Kiran, thought is the seed, but action… action is the soil, the water, and the sunlight. Without it, even the most divine seeds remain locked in possibility."

Guruji looked around at the others, then continued:

"Manifestation is not just the art of *thinking* clearly—it is the devotion of *moving* wisely. The Universe does not reward daydreams alone. It responds to your willingness to embody your prayer."

He paused, then smiled gently. "Let me tell you a story."

### The Story of the Weaver of Light

In a small Himalayan village lived a weaver—a quiet woman named **Maitreyi**. Each morning, she would sit before her loom and whisper a prayer into her thread:

*'Let this cloth bring warmth to those who feel forgotten.'*

But for years, she only dreamed of weaving a tapestry grand enough to cover the sacred shrine atop the distant peak—a tapestry that would shine like the morning sun and offer warmth to the spirit of the mountain.

Every night, she would see it in her mind—golden threads, dancing with symbols of light and compassion. She imagined pilgrims placing their heads upon it. She imagined even the wind slowing to kiss its sacred patterns.

But she never began.

Fear. Doubt. Busyness. The silent thefts of sacred time.

One day, as the village mourned the passing of an old monk, she saw him being carried up the mountain, wrapped in a coarse blanket. Tears welled up in her eyes. That night, she whispered to herself:

*'If not now... when? If not me... who?'*

The next morning, she began. One thread. One prayer. One breath at a time.

She rose before dawn. She worked through fatigue. She offered every weave like a mantra.

Months passed. Then a year. Then another. But finally, one morning, the villagers gathered as she climbed the sacred peak, now an elder herself. And there, upon the shrine, she unfolded her tapestry—not just of thread, but of devotion, intention, and **action**.

The cloth shimmered like sunlight captured in form.

And in that moment, the mountain didn't just receive warmth... it became witness to what a human soul could create when thought and action married in presence.

Guruji looked at Kiran with a still gaze—as if he were speaking not just to the man before him, but to the child within, who once dared to dream and hesitated to act.

"Intentions are the compass," he said softly, "but action is the step.

The Universe meets you not where you think, but where you move—with presence, with truth, with alignment."

He lifted a small copper pot beside him and poured water into a bowl.

"You can stare at this water all day, intending to quench your thirst. But until you lift it, bring it to your lips, and drink—the intention remains… only a whisper."

Guruji leaned slightly forward, his words now a gentle thunder.

"So move, Kiran. Move in the direction of your prayer. Let each act be a celebration of belief. Let every step say:

*'I trust life enough to participate in its unfolding.'*

'I am no longer waiting—I am weaving.'"

Kiran closed his eyes, and for a long time, didn't open them—not out of fatigue, but because something inside him was reweaving itself.

A quiet understanding passed through everyone present:

*Desires do not bloom where we only dream… they bloom where we begin.*

# CHAPTER XI

## The Sacred Practices of Manifestation

*"The journal is a sacred space where thoughts and dreams are crystallised into tangible paths. Write with clarity, for the universe follows the trail you lay with your pen."*

– Shree Shambav

### Synopsis

*This offering is a sacred invitation into a life of intention. It presents a curated collection of spiritual practices—daily rituals that anchor you in presence and purpose. From the quiet power of affirmations and guided meditations to the reflective clarity of vision journaling, gratitude practices, and frequency alignment, each ritual is designed to harmonise mind, body, and spirit with the essence of your highest desires.*

*These aren't merely tools for change—they are doorways into vibrational mastery. As you engage with them consistently, you begin to shift your inner frequency, attuning your energy field to the reality you seek to embody. In doing so, manifestation becomes less of a mystery and more of a natural unfolding—an echo of your inner alignment made visible.*

*This is a journey of conscious creation, where each breath, word, and intention becomes an act of sculpting your world from within. These sacred practices are not about escape; they are about returning—to your power, to your presence, and to the truth that you are always co-creating with the universe.*

## The Sacred Practices of Manifestation

The sun shimmered gently through the windows of Shambav Hall, casting a golden glow on the floor.

*Lalitha raised her hand and spoke with quiet clarity: "Guruji, how do daily affirmations strengthen the mind-body connection, and why is consistency essential for their power in manifestation?"*

Guruji closed his eyes for a moment. Then he opened them with a gaze full of presence and began:

"Lalitha, imagine a potter sitting before a wheel. He does not shape the clay with a single touch. Instead, his hands return again and again, gently but firmly, coaxing form out of the formless. Such is the power of daily affirmations. One utterance may pass through the mind like a breeze, but repetition—with awareness and feeling—becomes the hand that reshapes the clay of your inner world."

He continued, drawing the room into a hush.

"Your body listens to your thoughts. It doesn't merely react; it reflects. Every affirmation spoken with conviction becomes like a thread weaving the conscious and subconscious into alignment. But the weaving cannot be rushed."

Guruji paused, then leaned slightly forward, as though reading a sacred tale.

"Let me tell you a story," he said softly.

"There was once a woman named Meenakshi who lived on the edge of a dense forest. After years of illness and sorrow, she came to retreat with eyes dimmed by pain. 'Guruji,' she said, 'my body no longer listens to me. It's as though it has become someone else's.'

I said to her, 'Then speak to it like you would a beloved who's forgotten your voice.'

She looked puzzled. 'How do I begin?'

I handed her a diary and said, 'Every morning and every night, speak gently to your body. Tell it that it is loved. Tell it that it is healing. Tell it that it is whole. Even if it feels like a lie at first, speak until it remembers.'

She was diligent. For days, nothing changed. But on the 29th day, she told me something remarkable.

'Guruji,' she said with tears, 'I no longer feel like I'm lying when I say I'm healing. Something in me has started to believe again. It's as if my cells are listening now.'

By the third month, her posture changed. Her smile returned. Not because magic descended from the sky, but because the words she fed herself every day rewrote the chemistry of her hope.

"Her affirmations became like water to a wilted plant. Not a flood, but a faithful watering. And day by day, the garden of her inner world began to bloom."

## The Bridge Between Thought and Flesh

Guruji looked around the hall, his voice gentle but resolute.

"Your mind speaks in thought. Your body speaks in sensation. Affirmations are the translators. When spoken consistently—with breath, emotion, and presence—they carve new neural pathways. They are like travellers returning to the same village each day, until the path becomes a road and the road becomes a way of life."

He looked at Lalitha with a soft smile.

"Consistency is not repetition for the sake of habit—it is repetition for the sake of belief. You are not convincing the universe; you are remembering the truth you buried beneath years of doubt. And when the mind remembers, the body responds. The cells begin to dance in new rhythms, and that dance becomes your manifestation."

Guruji rose slowly and walked toward the small oil lamp flickering near the altar.

"Affirmations are not spells. They are invitations. Invitations to the divine within you to rise, to reawaken, to realign."

The hall was silent. The kind of silence that only comes when the heart is deeply stirred.

Lalitha bowed her head, tears shining in her eyes.

"Thank you, Guruji. I will begin again—with faith this time."

The golden light of morning filtered softly through the gauze curtains of Shambav Hall, casting long, peaceful shadows. A faint breeze rustled the leaves of the trees just beyond the open windows. The air was quiet, still charged with the energy of the earlier discussions. Birds chirped gently in the background, as if tuning in to the frequency of devotion.

*Nita, seated near the front, folded her hands and asked softly, "Guruji, what role does guided meditation play in creating a space for manifestation, and how can it be used to overcome mental blocks?"*

Guruji smiled, the corners of his eyes crinkling with warmth. He remained seated, his spine tall and his breath even.

**The Mirror Beneath the Lake**

"Nita," Guruji began, voice calm and grounding, "Have you ever seen your reflection in a disturbed pond?"

She shook her head gently.

"When the water is stirred, even by a light breeze, your reflection blurs. But when the water becomes still, even the smallest detail of your face shines back at you. The mind is no different. Guided meditation is the stilling of those inner waters. It is the gentle hand that calms the surface, allowing us to see ourselves—and our desires—clearly."

Guruji continued, glancing toward the far corner of the hall, as if seeing a memory in the air.

"Many years ago, a young woman named Amelia came here. Bright mind, devoted heart. But she felt stuck—no matter how many visualisations or intentions she set, her life never seemed to flow."

'Guruji,' she said to me one morning, just like this one, 'I believe in manifestation. But it's like something inside me… freezes. Every time I imagine my dream life, a voice whispers, *You don't deserve it.*'

I didn't offer answers. I guided her into silence.

Each morning, I led her through a gentle meditation. We didn't try to manifest anything at first. We just *listened*. We walked into the forest of her mind and sat beneath her fears like they were old trees. We acknowledged them. We bowed to them. We let them speak.

And then one day, in that silence, a buried memory surfaced— a teacher who once humiliated her when she dared to speak her dream aloud. That one moment had turned into a lifelong script.

But when it surfaced in stillness, it didn't control her anymore.

Amelia wept that morning. And in that tearful silence, the block dissolved."

## Why Guided Meditation Is Different

"You see," Guruji said, now looking around the hall at every soul present, "guided meditation is not just about relaxation. It is permission. It is permission to pause the noise of the outer world and step into the workshop of the soul. When done with consistency and reverence, it becomes the sacred bridge between intention and reality."

He lifted his hand slowly, as if tracing the arc of that bridge in the air.

"You do not manifest what you want—you manifest what you believe. And beliefs are not shifted by surface effort. They are transformed in the garden beneath the surface. Meditation is the spade that tills that garden."

**The Weaver's Loom**

Guruji closed his eyes briefly and spoke with a hushed depth:

"Imagine your mind as a loom. Every thought is a thread. But when thoughts tangle, the pattern is lost. Guided meditation is the weaver—untangling the knots, re-aligning the threads, restoring the beauty of the tapestry."

"And once that tapestry is woven with clarity, your reality cannot help but reflect it."

The room was silent. Even the birds outside seemed to hold their breath.

Nita's eyes glistened. "Thank you, Guruji," she whispered. "I understand now—meditation is not an escape from life. It is the space where life begins to take its truest shape."

Guruji nodded, his smile soft and radiant. *"And each morning, Nita, when you close your eyes with sincerity... that space becomes your sanctuary. That sanctuary becomes your reality."*


The subtle aroma of sandalwood lingered in the hall, dancing with the breeze that moved through the partially open windows. Birds could still be heard from the nearby banyan tree, as if listening in quiet reverence to the unfolding spiritual dialogue.

John raised his hand with a gentle gesture of curiosity and reverence.

*"Guruji,"* he asked, *"How can vision journaling help bridge the gap between our inner desires and our outer reality?"*

Guruji looked at John with kind eyes, nodding slowly. After a brief pause, he spoke.

**The Lantern and the Path**

"John," Guruji began, "Have you ever walked through a dense forest at dusk, holding only a small lantern?"

John nodded slightly.

"The path ahead cannot be seen in full. But the small circle of light from your lantern… that's enough. Step by step, that light guides you forward. Vision journaling is that lantern."

He paused, letting the image settle in everyone's hearts.

"You see, most people wander through life carrying a forest of thoughts but no light to guide them. Their desires remain like fog—present, but shapeless. But when you take a pen and journal, and begin to describe—not vaguely wish, but clearly articulate—your vision, your desires are no longer a mist. They become a map."

## A Dreamer in Disguise

Guruji leaned forward slightly, "Many years ago, a young man named Tom came to this very hall. A musician by heart, but bound by duties he did not choose. He worked in a government office, day after day, slowly shrinking into a version of himself he no longer recognised.

One morning, during a session on manifestation, I asked each person to write down their truest dream—not what they thought was possible, but what their soul ached for.

Tom hesitated. He had locked his dream away so tightly; he was afraid to speak it aloud.

But he returned the next day with a small notebook, worn at the edges, and said, 'Guruji, I've started. I write each morning now. I write as if I already live it—I see myself performing, I hear the applause, I even smell the wooden stage floor under my feet.'

And then," Guruji smiled, "a shift began."

Tom began waking up with more energy. His daily journaling wasn't just imagination—it was *preparation*. And slowly, life responded. A friend invited him to a local open mic. Then another. A producer heard him. Within a year, Tom was living the life he had only once dared to write.

He came to me months later and said, 'Guruji, it was like my words planted seeds in the soil of the universe. And now they've bloomed into reality.'"

## Why the Journal is Sacred

Guruji's voice deepened with reverence.

"Your journal is not just paper. It is a sacred altar. Each word you write is an offering. Each sentence, a prayer in motion. When you journal your vision consistently, with emotion and clarity, you are not begging the universe—you are communing with it. You are anchoring the invisible into form.

The law of attraction is not merely about 'wanting.' It is about *becoming*. And journaling makes you become familiar with the version of yourself that already has what you desire."

## The Architect Within

Guruji said, "An architect never builds without a blueprint. Even the tallest, most magnificent temple began as lines drawn on paper. Vision journaling is your blueprint. It aligns your thoughts, your energy, and your actions. And when all three move in harmony, reality cannot resist unfolding accordingly."

## A Pause of Silence

There was stillness in the hall. Some closed their eyes, no doubt already seeing themselves holding their own journals, sketching their deepest dreams, not as fantasies, but as inevitabilities.

John looked transformed—his gaze no longer questioning, but reflective. He pressed his palms together in gratitude.

"Thank you, Guruji," he whispered.

Guruji smiled.

"Write, John. Write not only to record what is, but to reveal what can be. For what you dare to write, you dare to believe. And what you dare to believe… life dares to deliver."

*Dev, his eyes carrying both inquiry and reverence. "Guruji," he began softly, "Why is frequency tuning vital in the manifestation process, and how can simple daily practices help elevate one's vibrational state to match their aspirations?"*

Guruji closed his eyes for a moment, as if tuning himself to a subtler realm. Then he opened them slowly, smiling—not just with his lips, but with an energy that seemed to wrap the hall in warmth.

**The Musician of the Universe**

"Dev," Guruji said gently, "Imagine the universe as an endless field of music. Everything—your thoughts, your emotions, your actions—emits a note. A vibration. A frequency. Now, if your dream vibrates at the frequency of joy, confidence, and abundance—but your thoughts hum with fear, doubt, or lack—you are playing the wrong tune."

Guruji paused and continued, "And when you're out of tune, the universe cannot hear you clearly. You must tune your instrument—your body, mind, and soul—so the symphony of your being matches the song of your desires."

Guruji leaned slightly forward as if drawing everyone closer. "There was a woman once—her name was Chinmayi. A gifted classical musician. But when her husband passed away suddenly, her music fell silent. Her home, once filled with morning ragas, grew heavy with grief. She packed her veena away and did not touch it for years.

When she came to the ashram, she told me, 'Guruji, I feel numb. My body moves, but I no longer live inside it.'

I asked her, 'When did your last prayer rise from the strings of your soul?'

She wept.

Then I said only this: 'Begin by tuning your veena again—just the strings, nothing more. No song, no performance. Just tuning.'

"And so she did. Every day. She sat by the river, tuning those strings. She still wouldn't play. But with each day, something changed. Her breath deepened. Her gaze softened. Her back straightened. It was as if the act of tuning her veena... was slowly tuning her soul."

One day, as the sun rose and birds cried out in praise, Chinmayi played a single note. And it reverberated—not just through the valley—but through her being.

And then the music returned. And so did her laughter, her appetite, her longing, her prayers.

She told me later, 'I didn't know tuning the veena would tune me. But it did.'"

**The Science of Spirit: Vibrational Truth**

Guruji now shifted into gentle explanation.

"Everything is energy, Dev. Your desires have a frequency. Your fear has a frequency. Your joy has a frequency. The universe responds not to your words, but to your vibration. You cannot trick the cosmos. You must become the thing you wish to receive."

**Simple Practices to Elevate Frequency**

Guruji looked at the whole gathering now.

"So how do we tune ourselves?" he asked, voice steady and kind.

He raised one finger.

- Breath: Conscious breathing is the string that connects body and spirit. Just ten minutes a day of mindful breathing can elevate your state."
- Sound: Chanting, singing, or listening to healing frequencies like 432 Hz or 528 Hz tunes your body like a temple instrument.
- Movement: Dance. Walk. Practice yoga. Let the energy move. Stagnation is the enemy of vibration.
- Gratitude: Nothing elevates your frequency faster than authentic, heartfelt gratitude. It is the purest song your heart can sing.
- Presence: Manifestation happens not in the past or future, but *now*. The more fully present you are, the clearer your vibration becomes.

Guruji then smiled.

"Your being is like a radio receiver. If you want to listen to classical music, you must tune to the right station. If you're stuck on static, don't curse the radio—adjust the dial. Your frequency is that dial. Manifestation is not about shouting louder; it's about tuning sharper."

**Closing Silence**

The hall fell into a sacred quiet. Dev's eyes were moist—whether from understanding or emotion, one couldn't say. Perhaps both.

He folded his hands and bowed his head.

"Thank you, Guruji," he whispered.

Guruji nodded with stillness.

*"Remember, Dev, the song you wish to hear from the universe is already playing. Your work is not to create it. Your work is to become the instrument that can receive it."*

The sun, casting warm fingers of light through the mist-veiled branches of Kumbhariyur's ancient banyan tree. It stood like a silent witness, its roots sprawling like veins of memory, embracing the earth, whispering to those who paused beneath it.

After the intense depth of the morning session in Shambav Hall, Guruji, with a soft smile and a pause heavy with meaning, had simply said: "Let us take a brief break."

The room exhaled. Some devotees lingered in contemplative silence, others moved toward the refreshment counter, and a few wandered out for a quiet stroll along the mud paths glistening under dew.

Near the banyan tree, a gathering naturally formed—Akshaya, Apeksha, Vaudeva, Kiran, and others drawn together not by schedule, but by shared silence. Vaudeva and Kiran moved about gently, handing out cups of steaming tea and coffee, the earthy aroma of cardamom and ginger mingling with the fresh morning air.

There was a sense of unspoken reverence. Everyone seemed to know that the break was not a break from learning—it was a continuation in a softer language.

Apeksha, always tender and poetic in her tone, held her cup gently, warming her hands. Her eyes wandered toward the stream that glimmered in the distance, just beyond the peepal grove. After a pause, she said quietly:

"Let me tell you all something... a story. It happened near that stream. A story of emotion... of pain... and how Guruji, in his stillness, dissolved what years of silence could not."

A hush descended. Even the breeze slowed to listen.

## The Story by the Stream – A Heart's Release

"It was about six years ago," Apeksha began, her voice carrying the soft gravity of memory.

"A young woman named Divyani came to our ashram. She was radiant in presence, but carried sorrow like a shadow stitched to her back.

No one knew her full story at first. She'd sit by that stream every morning, alone, staring into the water as if searching for something she'd lost.

Her eyes never smiled, even when her lips tried to. She was kind, generous, and helpful—yet unreachable, as though a part of her had shut its doors long ago."

Apeksha paused, taking a slow sip. Everyone listened, transfixed.

"One day, as she sat by the stream, Guruji approached. No words. No questions. He simply sat beside her. The water flowed. Birds chirped in indifference. Minutes passed. Then hours. Neither spoke.

And then... she began to cry. Not the kind of tears that fall from sorrow alone—but those that rise from recognition. From being seen.

She told him everything—how she had lost a child during childbirth. How everyone told her to 'move on.' How even her husband buried his grief in silence.

She felt invisible. Hollow. Angry at herself. At God. She stopped believing that healing was even possible."

Apeksha's voice caught for a moment. The group sat motionless.

"Guruji didn't offer advice that day. He just listened, as if her words were sacred scripture.

When she finished, he picked up a leaf that had floated down onto the water.

'This leaf,' he said, 'was once part of a great tree. It served its time. Now it floats—not lost, but free. Your grief isn't something to suppress. It's something to honour. Let it float. Not to forget, but to release.'

He placed the leaf back on the stream. It drifted, slowly but surely, down the current, glistening in the light."

**From Pain to Presence**

Apeksha now looked around the circle.

"Since that day, Divyani changed. She still remembered her child, but with gentleness. She started singing again. She laughed. Not to hide pain—but because she no longer feared it.

Guruji didn't just give her words. He gave her **permission**. To feel. To break. To rise again—not as who she was, but as who she could become."

The story settled in the hearts around her like incense in a quiet temple.

Kiran whispered, "So sometimes... healing is not about fixing, but allowing."

Apeksha smiled. "Exactly. That is Guruji's way. He doesn't fix you. He sits with you... until you remember that you were never broken."

**The Bell and the Call**

Just then, the gentle chime of the bell rang from the Shambav Hall—soft yet unmistakable. A call, not just to return, but to continue.

Devotees rose slowly, some in silence, others with thoughtful nods. Eyes met briefly—acknowledging the weight and gift of what was just shared.

As they walked back toward the hall, Akshaya turned back once to look at the banyan tree.

It stood still, timeless, like Guruji himself—a silent shelter, a keeper of stories, a witness to the sacred unravelling of human hearts.

# PART FOUR

## Manifestation in Everyday Life

*"Every relationship you attract is a reflection of the love, respect, and truth you hold within yourself."*

-Shree Shambav

# CHAPTER XII

## Manifestation

*"The body listens to the whispers of the mind and heart—manifest your health by nourishing both with love, belief, and alignment."*

– Shree Shambav

### Synopsis

*This section delves into the all-encompassing nature of manifestation and how its principles ripple into every facet of life—relationships, health, wealth, and purpose. It reveals how the power of focused intention, energetic alignment, and emotional awareness can become the foundation for true transformation. As you learn to harness these inner forces, you begin to witness their outer reflections: deeper and more meaningful connections, vibrant physical well-being, a natural flow of financial abundance, and a growing clarity of purpose that brings lasting peace. Manifestation is not confined to one realm of life—it is a holistic way of being, where every thought, feeling, and action becomes part of the sacred art of conscious creation.*

### Manifestation in Relationships, Health, Wealth, and Purpose

*Akshatha asked, "Guruji, why do we resist change, even when it is necessary?"*

Guruji closed his eyes for a moment, as if reaching into a deeper space of remembrance, and then gently opened them with a soft smile.

The golden hue of sunlight filtered softly through the carved wooden panels of Shambav Hall. The session was gently unfolding like a sacred lotus—each petal a question, each answer a drop of truth falling into the still pond of the seekers' hearts.

After Kiran's question on aligned action, there was a pause—not of silence, but of anticipation. It was then that Sam, sitting near the eastern window where the breeze still carried the coolness, stood up slowly.

His voice held a mix of vulnerability and courage.

*"**Guruji,**" he began, "How can we use manifestation to create deeper and more authentic connections in our personal relationships?*

*Can our intention and energy truly shape the love we receive, the trust we build, and the emotional depth we experience with others?"*

The room stilled further, as if even the trees outside leaned in to listen. Guruji looked at Sam, his eyes soft but focused.

## The Mirror of the Heart

"Ah, Sam," Guruji said with a gentle nod. "You have touched the essence of what it means to manifest—not just objects or outcomes, but intimacy, resonance, and connection.

To manifest love, we must become love. To attract depth, we must first be willing to dwell there ourselves."

He closed his eyes briefly, drawing in a slow breath, as if inviting the universe to speak through him.

"Relationships are not found—they are remembered. They are echoes of the frequency we hold within ourselves. You do not attract what you *desire*...

**You attract what you are ready for.**"

## A Manifestation of Mirrors

Guruji said, "There once lived a man named Jayarama, a skilled carpenter in a quiet village not unlike this one. His hands-built temples for others, but his own heart remained an unfinished house.

He longed for a partner—someone who could see through his silences, someone with whom love would feel like returning home.

One night, under a starlit sky, he whispered into the wind:

*'If there is someone for me, let her find me in truth, not pretence. Let her see my cracks and not flinch.'*

Days passed. Months. But instead of searching endlessly, Jayarama turned inward. He began to live as if she were already in his life—not in delusion, but in devotion.

He would speak gently to himself. He would set a place at dinner for her spirit. He would sit beneath the banyan tree and read aloud, as though her laughter was just beyond the rustling leaves.

And then, one morning, Sasikala arrived in the village—an artist, a wanderer, a woman whose silence felt like a familiar prayer.

They met not with fireworks, but with a stillness that said: I've known you before.

Not because they were lucky. But because they had become the people who could truly meet each other."


**The Inner Work of Relating**

Guruji looked back at Sam.

"You see, manifestation in relationships is not about scripting someone else's role. It's about becoming the vibration of the relationship you seek.

*If you want to be seen—stop hiding from yourself.*

*If you want to be heard—start honouring your own voice.*

*If you long for trust—begin by trusting your own heart, your own healing.*

Energy speaks louder than words. When you shift your frequency from fear to self-love, from scarcity to openness—you stop attracting people who mirror your wounds and start attracting those who mirror your readiness for wholeness."

He then lifted a small mirror from beside his seat, polished with sandalwood oil, and held it up.

"This," he said, "is what life gives you. A mirror. If you frown, it frowns back. If you smile, it smiles. But if you gaze with love…

The mirror becomes a window—and suddenly, you're not just looking at yourself, you're looking into another soul who is looking into you."

## The Seed and the Soil

"Relationships," Guruji continued, "are gardens. Manifestation is the seed, but your thoughts, intentions, and actions—they are the soil and water.

*You cannot plant love in a heart full of resentment.*

*You cannot grow trust in a mind clouded with doubt.*

Manifestation begins the moment you stop waiting for another to complete you, and begin cultivating the completeness within."

He looked around the hall, his voice softer now, almost like a prayer.

"To manifest authentic connection, you must live in alignment with the kind of love you wish to receive. Be the friend, the partner, the listener, the truth-teller… not because someone else deserves it, but because *you* do."

Sam sat down slowly, his eyes glistening not just with understanding, but with a quiet resolve. Something had shifted—not outside, but inside.

And in that sacred space, everyone felt the truth settle deep in their bones:

*Love is not summoned. It is remembered. And it begins… always… with the self.*

The sacred stillness in Shambav Hall continued to cradle the seekers like the arms of a mother holding her child before it learns to walk again. The golden light filtering through the open windows made the wooden floor shimmer, as if the space itself was listening with reverence.

After Sam's question on relationships had stirred silent reflection, Alice, draped in a soft maroon shawl, stood up with gentleness but unmistakable urgency in her voice.

*"Guruji,"* Alice said, *"in what ways can manifestation principles contribute to improving physical health and well-being? Can our thoughts, beliefs, and emotional energies shape how our body heals, thrives, or deteriorates?"*

The question did not fall. It floated—tender, weighty, and intimate.

Guruji's gaze settled on Alice with the softness of moonlight on still water. He placed his hand over his heart and took a breath—not to prepare his answer, but to honour the depth from which the question had come.

**The Body as a Living Prayer**

"Alice," Guruji said, his voice warm like the first sip of water after a fast,

*"Your body is not a machine to be fixed—it is a garden that responds to how it is tended.*

*Every thought is a seed. Every emotion is rain or drought.*

*Every belief is the sunlight or the shadow beneath which that garden either blooms… or withers."*

He paused, letting those words settle into the sacred hush.

"Most people treat healing as an external battle—medicine versus illness, treatment versus symptoms.

But healing is more than the absence of pain.

*True well-being begins within—where the soul whispers to the cells, 'You are safe now. You may thrive.'"*

## Healing Beyond the Physical

Guruji, after a pause, said, "Let me tell you the story of Devika, a young woman once riddled with fatigue, chronic illness, and despair. Doctors gave her labels. Pills dulled the symptoms, but nothing changed the emptiness she felt inside—until one day, when her grandfather, a quiet yogi, asked her a strange question: 'Devika, when was the last time you told your body that you loved it?'

She laughed at first. How could love heal something that biology had already condemned?

But something in her stirred. And so, she began—timidly at first—with daily affirmations whispered before sleep:

*'I am healing. I am whole. I forgive you, body, for hurting. I thank you, body, for staying.'*

Then came the visualisation. She imagined her immune cells not as warriors, but as gardeners, gently pruning, watering, mending.

*She changed her words from 'fighting disease' to 'inviting harmony.'*

*She began to eat not from fear of illness, but in celebration of life.*

*She wrote letters of apology to the parts of her body she had shamed.*

*Slowly… not magically, but miraculously… the pain lessened. Energy returned. Joy found its way back into her mornings.*

Her healing didn't come from manifestation—it came through it. She realigned with the wisdom that her body was never the enemy. It was simply waiting for her to return… with love."

**Your Body Listens**

"You see, Alice," Guruji continued, "your body is the most loyal listener you'll ever have. It eavesdrops on your thoughts, responds to your emotions, and records your beliefs like mantras etched into its very tissues.

When you constantly think: I am sick, I am broken, your body hears, 'This is the reality I must maintain.'But when you declare with emotional clarity: I am healing. I am vibrant. I trust in my body's wisdom; you begin to whisper a new blueprint into your biology."

Guruji looked around the hall, his eyes shimmering with emotion.

"Manifestation is not denial of illness—it is the **invocation of wholeness.**

It is meeting the body not with fear, but with partnership.

The cells respond to hope. The heart listens to belief. And the nervous system is calmed not just by medicine, but by meaning."

## The River and the Vessel

Guruji then picked up a small brass kalash filled with water, holding it in both hands.

*"Imagine this water is your life force. Your thoughts are the riverbanks guiding its flow. If your inner dialogue is filled with fear, guilt, or shame—it leaks.*

*But if you build it with intention, with gratitude, with gentleness—it holds. It flows. It nourishes."*

Guruji poured a little water into the small tulsi plant at the corner of the hall.

*"Your body is not a battlefield. It is a temple, and every thought is an offering. What will you place on its altar today?"*

Alice sat down slowly, her breath deepened, as if some ancient part of her had remembered what modern life had made her forget:

**The body does not just carry us. It speaks, it feels, it remembers—and, most of all, it responds to love.**

*It was then that Bhavya, her voice steady, "Guruji," she asked, "what role does manifestation play in attracting financial abundance and creating a flow of wealth?*

*Can intention, belief, and alignment truly influence our prosperity in the material world?"*

A silence followed—not heavy, but rich, like the pause before rain touches the earth. Many others shifted slightly. The topic of money—often shrouded in guilt, scarcity, or shame—had entered sacred space. And yet, Guruji smiled, as though he had been waiting for this question to arrive.

**Money as a Mirror of Inner Worth**

"Bhavya," Guruji began gently, "money is not dirty. It is not divine. It is **neutral**—a mirror, reflecting the beliefs we hold, the energy we emit, and the value we place on our own being."

He held up a silver coin, light glinting from its edge.

"This coin is lifeless until we assign it meaning.

For some, it brings anxiety. For others, opportunity. And for a few, it is a sacred trust—a current that flows through their life to uplift not only themselves but others."


**From Scarcity to Sacred Flow**

Guruji's eyes sparkled as he began one of his cherished parables:

"There was once a young sculptor named Arun, who lived in a small village. Though his work was exquisite, he struggled—barely selling a piece each month. He believed artists must suffer. That money corrupted purity. That wealth and wisdom could not coexist.

One day, an old traveller visited and admired his sculptures. 'Why do you hide such beauty behind fear?' the traveller asked.

Arun replied, 'I create from love, not for coins. I do not chase wealth.'

The traveller smiled. 'But what if wealth is also an expression of love? What if money is not the enemy, but a messenger—bringing your gift to those who need it, and returning energy to sustain your journey?'

That night, Arun couldn't sleep. Something shifted.

He began carving not just with passion, but with intention. Each morning, he'd declare:

*"I am worthy of prosperity. My art blesses others. Abundance flows to me as I give from my soul."*

He visualised patrons smiling as they received his work. He wrote down financial goals not from greed, but with clarity and joy.

And slowly, things changed. Commissions came. Exhibits were offered. But more than the outer wealth, it was his relationship with money that transformed—from resistance to reverence."

## Manifestation and Financial Energy

"Bhavya," Guruji continued, "money is a form of energy exchange. When you align your intentions with service, clarity, and worthiness, you stop chasing money—and start attracting flow."

He looked around the hall, then added:

"Most people repel abundance not because they don't work hard, but because they secretly believe:

*'I'm not worthy.'*

*'It's wrong to want more.'*

*'Rich people are selfish.'*

*'I'll lose myself in success.'*

These thoughts become the invisible locks on the doors of prosperity."

Guruji drew a gentle analogy:

"Imagine a river. If you fear its flow, you build dams. If you doubt it, you dig escape channels. But if you trust it—you build bridges, boats, and gardens along its banks.

Money, like the river, must move. To hoard is to stagnate. To fear is to block. But to align with it—consciously, lovingly—is to let it serve its purpose."

## The Practical Path

Guruji then offered this with warmth:

"Manifesting wealth is not sitting idly and wishing for gold to fall from the sky. It is about aligning belief, clarity, emotion, and action:

1. **Affirm your worth**: *I am open to receive. I am worthy of abundance.*

2. **Visualise in detail**: Feel the freedom, peace, and joy that wealth brings.

3. **Release scarcity**: Let go of guilt or shame attached to money.

4. **Serve with value**: Create, offer, or work from a space of authenticity.

5. **Gratitude is magnetic**: Appreciate every small inflow—it expands the channel.

6. **Bless others' abundance**: Envy blocks. Blessing expands."

Guruji smiled.

"When your soul is aligned, and your energy is clean, the Universe doesn't just send you money—it sends you means, ideas, synchronicities, people, and purpose.

Prosperity becomes not a chase, but a **dance**."

Bhavya's eyes welled up—not from sadness, but from the recognition that her old story of struggle could finally be rewritten.

As the wind stirred the chimes near the entrance, the sound whispered like a secret:

*"You are not meant to survive. You are meant to thrive."*

As Guruji's eyes moved across the room, they paused on Aarna. There was a subtle tremor in her tone, not of fear, but of longing—the kind of longing that comes not from the mind but the soul.

*"Guruji," she asked, "How can manifestation help us align with our true life's purpose and experience inner peace?"*

## The Inner Compass and the Outer Journey

Guruji nodded gently, "Aarna," he said softly, "to ask about your purpose is to already be walking toward it.

For purpose is not something we find—

It's something we **remember**."

The air grew deeper. The wind outside rustled the trees like an unseen hand whispering through leaves.

## The Weaver Who Forgot

Guruji began, with a story—one that unwrapped its message like a lotus blooming slowly.

"In a distant village nestled among blue hills, lived a girl named Shobha. She was born into a family of weavers—people who turned threads into magic. Her fingers were gifted, and her soul even more so.

But as years passed, Shobha's father fell ill, and the family struggled. In the chaos, her loom gathered dust. Neighbours advised her to 'be practical,' and she took up work at a nearby mine, digging stone instead of weaving dreams.

Each evening, her heart ached. But she convinced herself it was 'just life.'

One day, an old woman arrived in the village, wearing a shawl of breathtaking beauty—one Shobha immediately recognised. It was her own work, from years ago. The woman said, *'I bought this in the city. It brought me warmth on my darkest days. Who made this?'*

In that moment, Shobha wept. Not from pride, but from remembering—who she really was. That night, she dusted off her loom and lit a lamp. She whispered, 'I was not born to break stone. I was born to weave soul into thread.'"

**A Sacred Returning**

Guruji looked into Aarna's eyes.

"Manifestation is not just about creating the life you want—it is about unveiling the life you were born for.

It is the art of aligning your thoughts, feelings, and actions with the quiet whisper that has always been within."

Guruji continued:

"Most people search for purpose in job titles, social approval, or outer success. But true purpose lives not in what we *do*, but in who we *are* when we feel **most alive**.

And so, we begin with questions, not answers:

- *What brings me deep peace when no one is watching?*
- *What do I lose myself in, and find my Self again?*
- *What am I afraid to admit I truly desire?*

These questions are seeds. Manifestation is the sunlight."

**The Pathway of Alignment**

Guruji offered a gentle roadmap:

1. **Clarity of Desire** – "Your soul already knows. Sit in silence. Listen. Let your longing rise without judgment."

2. **Visualisation as Compass** – "Picture a life that feels like freedom, not pressure. What does your day look like? Who are you becoming?"

3. **Affirm with Emotion** – "Affirm: *I am in harmony with my sacred path. I allow purpose to reveal itself through peace.*"

4. **Follow Inspired Action** – "When you feel a pull—toward a book, a person, a calling—honour it. That's your compass turning."

5. **Trust the Timing** – "Just as a seed does not bloom by force, your purpose unfolds not by pushing, but by presence."

## The River and the Ocean

Guruji leaned forward slightly, "Imagine a river, Aarna. It doesn't strain to reach the ocean. It flows—trusting the current. It curves when it must, slows in silence, rushes with joy.

Your purpose is not a destination. It is your **nature**. It is where your deepest love meets the world's greatest need.

When your inner stream aligns with that truth, peace is not something you search for. It becomes the **water you swim in**."

A hush fell over Shambav Hall. Aarna's eyes shimmered—not from confusion, but clarity. Not from doubt, but devotion.

She did not speak again. She didn't need to. Her silence now spoke of an inner vow being made—not to chase purpose, but to surrender to it.

### Guruji, after a pause, said:

"The greatest manifestation is not gold or fame.

It is to wake each morning, breathe deeply, and say—

*'I am exactly where I am meant to be. I am becoming who I was born to be.'*

That is peace. That is the purpose. That is the path."

After the morning's intensity and silence, a long pause settled over Shambav Hall, like the breath between two heartbeats.

Guruji sat still, eyes gently closed. Then, with a voice as calm as flowing water, he opened his eyes and said:

"Let us break for lunch now, my dear ones. We will gather again here at five."

With that, the room stirred gently to life. The devotees slowly rose from their asanas, their movements unhurried, as though still immersed in the echoes of the morning's wisdom. Some headed toward their rooms to refresh and reflect, while others followed the inviting aroma wafting from the Food Mall, where a lovingly prepared afternoon meal awaited—simple, sattvic, yet nourishing to body and soul.

The laughter of birds mingled with the soft chime of bells from the nearby shrine as the ashram slowly exhaled into the rhythm of the afternoon.

Among the gentle bustle, Nita and Padma, with a sense of quiet initiative, gathered their friends and said with a smile,

"Let's meet near the stream once lunch is done. There's more to reflect upon… more to feel."

And so it was. The small group gathered by the stream—its crystal waters murmuring softly like an eternal hymn.

There sat Abhirami, Kiran, Sam, Alice, Sofia, Bhavya, Aarna, and a few others—each one still carrying the sacred silence of the morning within, now ready to process, ponder, and share.

Sam stretched his legs out over the sun-warmed grass and smiled,

"We've got time until five… enough to swim through a few stories."

Alice chuckled as she leaned back against a tree trunk,

"Then surely Apeksha will take us on a journey… her tales always find the hidden doorways to the heart."

Astyn nodded quietly. Her eyes sparkled with anticipation. Kieron added, "There's something about the way she tells them… like she doesn't just remember the stories—she feels them for us."

Heads turned, and as if summoned by intention, Apeksha arrived, serene as always. Her footsteps made no sound, and yet her presence spoke louder than words. She settled onto a large stone near the bank of the stream. The leaves rustled as though greeting her.

She looked at them, one by one, and then at the stream that wound through the ashram like a silver thread stitching time and memory together. She said nothing at first. Just sat. Then, after a long, soul-filled pause, she began.

"There are many stories," she said, "but today, let me tell you three that still whisper through the corners of my mind. They are not stories of miracles—but of quiet transformations. Of how Guruji, with a glance, a word, or sometimes no word at all, changed the trajectory of a soul."

Apeksha said, "The First Story: His name was Raghavan. A quiet man in his fifties with tired eyes that had forgotten how to shine. He had come to the ashram not for spiritual curiosity, but out of desperation—haunted by a mistake he had made two decades ago.

He sat before Guruji one dusky evening in the meditation grove, the scent of jasmine in the air and the cicadas just beginning their twilight song.

"Guruji," he whispered, his voice strained, "I cannot forgive myself. I wronged someone I loved. And though they forgave me… I never could."

Guruji looked at him for a long moment. No judgment. No pity. Just presence. Then, he reached for the wooden table beside him and handed Raghavan a blank page and a fountain pen.

"Write," Guruji said.

"Write what?" Raghavan asked, confused.

"Write your pain. Write until your heart runs out of ink. Let the page carry what your soul has carried too long."

Each morning, Raghavan sat by the river and wrote—sometimes in sentences, other times just words, sometimes in angry scribbles. Pages filled with memories, regrets, and apologies never spoken aloud.

Four days passed. On the fifth, he came with a small pile of folded pages.

"It's all here," he told Guruji, eyes brimming.

Guruji nodded and walked with him silently to the edge of the river. With trembling hands, Raghavan set the papers aflame.

As the ashes danced into the wind, something shifted in him—a heaviness lifted, not forcibly, but like a bird slowly rising after years in a cage.

"You didn't need a pardon," Guruji said, "you needed release."

Apeksha continued the Second Story: Her name was Saraswati. Young—no more than thirty—but her eyes held the weight of many lifetimes. Her husband had passed in a tragic accident, leaving her with a void so vast she could no longer see herself.

She arrived at the ashram wearing white, speaking little, and always sitting at the far back of every gathering. She believed her life had ended with her husband's.

One night, under a full moon, the ashram gathered for satsang. The fire crackled. The sky shimmered. And Guruji, seeing Saraswati's unspoken grief, paused his teaching.

He looked directly at her, and with the gentlest voice, said:

"The soul's journey doesn't end in the silence of death, but in the silence, you are afraid to enter."

Saraswati looked up, startled. She had never spoken to him directly before. But those words pierced through her numbness.

"Silence has been my curse," she said, voice quivering.

"No," Guruji replied. "Silence is not absence. It is presence… without noise. Let it speak to you."

From that night on, Saraswati stopped fearing silence. She began walking barefoot at dawn, listening to the wind, sitting by the peepal tree, feeling its stillness. She started sketching again—something she hadn't done since her husband died. Her grief did not vanish, but it softened. It became a companion instead of a chain.

Months later, during another satsang, she recited a poem she had written, her voice steady:

"I searched for him in sound…

But found him in silence."

Apeksha, after a brief pause, said, "The Third Story: Her name was Nimisha—a little girl of seven with eyes like galaxies and lips that had never spoken a word. She was brought to the ashram by her parents, desperate and worn after years of therapies and diagnoses."

But Guruji didn't ask for a diagnosis. He didn't ask her to speak.

Instead, he asked the ashram to **listen**—truly listen—not with ears, but with heart. Whenever Nimisha was around, Guruji would say:

"Watch her eyes. They speak. Her silence is not lack—it is language."

She became everyone's teacher. People slowed down around her, knelt to her level, and smiled without needing reasons. She painted, she laughed soundlessly, she moved like light itself. And slowly, her presence began to stir a shift in the community. They listened more, judged less.

One morning, during a musical meditation, the harmonium played a gentle raga, and a miracle unfolded.

Nimisha began to hum.

Then her hum became a melody.

Then her melody became a song.

Everyone froze. No one moved. No one dared interrupt the divine.

Her first word was not spoken.

It was sung.

And not one soul in the room doubted they had just witnessed something far beyond a child finding her voice—it was grace, made audible.

Later, Guruji simply said:

"Sometimes silence is not broken. It is translated."

As Apeksha finished, a deep stillness settled over the group. Not the silence of nothingness—but the silence after something sacred has passed through.

Moments later, the group stood and slowly began making their way toward the refreshment centre. Steam rose from the cups of tea and coffee as laughter and reflection intertwined, warm in the golden light. Even the breeze seemed sweeter now.

And then, from the distant Shambav Hall, the bell rang again—a soft, clear note calling them back. Not to continue something... but to deepen it.

They looked at each other and smiled. No one needed to speak.

With hearts a little fuller and eyes a little softer, they made their way toward the hall—where the journey would not start again, but simply unfold further, like a lotus in patient bloom.

# PART FIVE

## The Manifestor's Lifestyle

*"You are not a passive observer of life's unfolding; you are a creator, co-designing every moment with the universe's infinite intelligence."*

- *Shree Shambav*

# CHAPTER XIII

## Living as a Manifestor

*"Manifestation is not a single act but the art of living consciously every day, knowing that every thought, every emotion, and every action shapes your reality."*

– Shree Shambav

### Synopsis

Manifestation is not a one-time process, but a continuous journey that becomes a way of life. In this final chapter, readers are guided to integrate the principles of manifestation into their daily lives, not just as an occasional practice, but as a state of being. Living as a manifestor means aligning with purpose, embracing the flow of life, and cultivating a mindset of gratitude and self-love. It encourages readers to trust the process, stay present, and engage with life fearlessly, knowing that they are always co-creating their reality in every moment. By adopting a life of intentionality and cosmic alignment, the reader can truly step into their power as a creator and manifest a life filled with purpose and fulfilment.

### Living as a Manifestor—A Life of Purpose and Flow

The golden sun was slowly descending behind the distant hills, casting long shadows across the Shambav ashram. The air was gentle, scented faintly with sandalwood and jasmine. Birds began their homeward flight, painting soft arcs in the amber sky. The day had matured into a moment of stillness, where even time seemed to pause in reverence.

Devotees had quietly returned to Shambav Hall after the break, their hearts calmed by nature's soft symphony. The hall was soaked in twilight silence, interrupted only by the rustle of robes and the sound of quiet breaths.

Guruji, seated on his asana, radiated an aura of silent strength. His eyes, half-closed, opened slowly as Rohith rose from his seat.

*"Guruji,"* Rohith asked, his voice gentle yet steady, *"How can embracing manifestation as a lifestyle shift our perception of challenges and obstacles in life?"*

Guruji looked toward the window, where the last light of the day touched the banyan leaves. Then, turning his gaze to the gathering, he spoke:

### The River and the Rock

Guruji said, "Let me narrate a story. Long ago, in a village nestled by a mountain stream, there lived a potter named Viren. He was known not only for shaping clay into exquisite vessels, but also for the weight he carried in his heart. You see, every time life placed a rock in his path—a failed sale, a broken kiln, a lost love—he cursed the heavens and hardened his heart. 'Why me?' he would ask, never receiving an answer he liked.

One day, after a particularly painful season of drought, Viren walked to the stream, hoping to gather water for his weary body. But the stream had narrowed to a trickle. Frustrated, he hurled a stone into the little streambed, shouting, 'Again, an obstacle!'

Just then, an old woman, bent with age and grace, appeared beside him. She smiled and pointed at the same rock he had thrown. 'Look again,' she said.

Over the weeks, Viren returned to the stream. He saw how the water, though gentle, kept flowing. The rock remained, but the water didn't resist—it danced around it. Eventually, it polished it. The obstacle became part of the beauty of the flow.

And slowly, something shifted in Viren. He began to see that the rock was not against the water. It was the teacher of the water's dance."

Guruji paused, letting the silence hold the lesson.

"Rohith," Guruji continued, his voice deepening, "Manifestation is not about controlling life so it becomes smooth. It is about flowing with intention, trust, and clarity, like the stream. When you embrace manifestation as a lifestyle—not as a tool to 'fix' life but as a way of being—every obstacle becomes a message, a sculptor, a mirror."

He looked around the hall, now washed in the hues of dusk.

"The universe doesn't punish. It aligns. Challenges are not punishments; they are frequency checks. When you see difficulties as invitations to realign with your highest truth, you stop resisting and start responding. That shift—from victimhood to conscious creation—is where true manifestation begins.

So ask not 'Why me?' but 'What in me is ready to grow?' And you will see, the rock is not in your way. It is on your path."

Rohith folded his hands, eyes glistening. Around him, others sat in quiet stillness, their hearts moved not just by words but by the gentle evening that seemed to whisper the same wisdom through the trees.

A koel called in the distance. The sun disappeared beyond the horizon, and lights lit the hall. A new light, inward and timeless, had also been kindled.

A few heartbeats of silence passed—pregnant, alive.

Then Sujitha raised her voice gently, her eyes glowing with curiosity and reverence.

*"Guruji, what does it mean to live in 'flow' with the universe? And how can we cultivate this flow to enhance our manifestations?"*

Guruji turned his gaze to her, eyes reflecting the subtle glow of both lamp and flame. He remained quiet for a few seconds longer, and then his voice emerged—measured, grounded, gentle.

"To live in flow, Sujitha, is not to push the current, but to surrender to it. Flow is not passivity. It is powerful alignment."

He gestured subtly toward the *Jyoti* in the corner.

"That flame does not burn with resistance. It doesn't fight the air around it. It dances. That is the essence of flow. It trusts the fuel provided, the stillness of the space, the sacredness of its purpose."

Guruji leaned forward slightly.

"Most people are swimming against the river of life. They try to force doors open, control outcomes, and resist what is. But the universe isn't a machine to be operated. It is a symphony to be attuned to. When you are in flow, you don't chase your destiny... you magnetise it."

### The Bamboo and the Wind

"There was once a man named Keshava who lived near a forest," Guruji began. "He was a skilled woodcutter—strong, focused, disciplined. Every morning, he would march into the woods with his axe, carving his way through life, shaping everything with force and will. He believed in hard work. In an effort. In control.

One summer, a great storm hit the region. Trees were uprooted, branches snapped, and the very forest trembled. When Keshava walked through the woods the next morning, he was stunned. Mighty oaks had fallen. Proud sal trees lay broken. But deep within the forest, untouched and swaying gently in the breeze, stood a grove of bamboo.

He stood before them, confused. 'Why are they the only ones left standing?' he asked aloud.

An old monk who had taken refuge nearby smiled and said, 'Because they know how to bow. They bend with the wind, not against it.'

That moment marked the beginning of Keshava's true journey."

Guruji said, "Let me narrate a story: Nandan, a young sculptor who had come to the ashram a few years ago, was bitter with disappointment.

Nandan had tried every strategy, every tool, every technique. Still, nothing worked. His art felt lifeless, and his dreams crumbled in his hands like dry clay.

"I told him," Guruji said, "to take no chisel, no sketchbook—only his presence. For twenty-one days, he was to walk the gardens, sit beside the stream, and simply observe. No striving. Just sensing. Just being."

At first, Nandan struggled. But then, on the eleventh day, he noticed the rhythm of a falling leaf. On the fifteenth, he began to hear the music of the wind. On the twenty-first, he wept beside the river—not because of what he had created, but because of what he had become.

"On the twenty-second day," Guruji said softly, "he picked up the chisel again. This time, not to sculpt the world—but to let the world sculpt through him."

The hall remained still, the warmth of the electric lights wrapping the room in softness, and the divine flame flickering in its corner, bearing silent testimony.

The Weaver's Loom

"Imagine," Guruji continued, "a grand loom on which the universe is weaving a tapestry. Every thread you pull with intention, every emotion you offer with faith, becomes part of the design. But if you pull with fear, or force, the pattern distorts. The weaver must pause, unpick the knots, and try again."

"To stay in flow," he said, "is to trust the weaver."

"You cultivate this by surrendering the need to control the 'how' and deepening your relationship with the 'why.' You flow when you stay present, when you let inspired action lead instead of anxious effort, when you remember that sometimes, pausing is progress and silence is alignment."

"Flow," Guruji said, "is when the doer becomes the dancer, when you move without resistance. You align. You surrender. And in that surrender, you awaken the most powerful creative force within you."

Guruji looked around the hall, his voice now a whisper.

*"To live in flow is to live with trust. With rhythm. With grace. And to allow the universe to use your hands as its own."*

*Astyn, her voice tender and sincere asked: "Guruji, how do gratitude and self-love serve as the foundation for successful manifestation and a fulfilling life?"*

A long pause.

Then Guruji opened his eyes, his gaze resting gently on Astyn.

"Astyn," he began, "gratitude is the language of the soul. Self-love is the breath it takes to stay alive."

He leaned forward slightly, eyes glinting like embers.

"To manifest a life of meaning and beauty without these two is like trying to draw water from a dry well."

Guruji looked to the divine flame and said softly:

"Would you pour blessings into a vessel that leaks? The universe is generous, but it waits until the heart becomes a container worthy of receiving. Gratitude seals the cracks of doubt. Self-love strengthens the walls from within."

**The Woman Who Could Not See Her Light**

Guruji said, "Let me narrate a story: There was once a woman named Chandrika, a teacher by profession and a giver by nature. She had spent years pouring herself into the lives of others—her students, her parents, even strangers. People often called her "angelic." But when alone, Chandrika felt invisible, unworthy, and strangely unfulfilled.

She came to the ashram during a winter retreat, sitting always in the back row, smiling gently but never speaking. Until one morning, during a walking meditation, she broke down in tears beside the *Tulsi* altar.

Guruji found her there, crumpled, whispering words she didn't know she was still holding inside:

"Why am I never enough for myself?"

Guruji didn't answer. Instead, he handed her a small, hand-carved mirror from his satchel. On its back was etched a single word: **"Pratyaksha"**—*self-revealed*.

"For forty days," he said, "each morning before sunrise, go to the lake and sit with this mirror. Say one thing you're grateful for. And one thing you love about yourself. Even if it feels like a lie."

The first day, she stared at the mirror, unable to speak. Her voice broke. Her lips trembled. Her reflection looked like a stranger.

But she returned the next day. And the next. Her words came in whispers—*I am grateful for my breath. I love my patience.* Small things. Honest things. On day fifteen, she said with a smile, *I love my eyes—they have seen so much pain, yet still look for light.*

By day forty, she did not bring the mirror at all.

When Guruji met her on the final day, she was simply sitting by the lake, the sunrise reflecting in her moist eyes.

"I no longer need to see my reflection," she said. "I have become it."

Guruji turned again to the devotees.

"You see, Astyn, when you practice gratitude, you shift your energy from lack to abundance. You begin to notice the invisible threads of grace that already surround you. And when you love yourself—not egoically, but tenderly—you vibrate with wholeness. You tell the universe: 'I am ready to receive because I have already found gold within.'"

He gestured toward the divine flame in the corner of the hall.

"That flame burns not because we demand it to. It burns because someone cared enough to tend to it, to love it, to offer it reverence. So too, your inner light. Gratitude is the matchstick. Self-love is the oil. Together, they ignite the fire of manifestation."

Guruji's voice softened to a whisper.

"Without these, manifestation becomes wishful thinking. With them, it becomes divine magnetism."


Roopa her voice was steady but shadowed with longing.

*"Guruji," she asked, "What role does fearlessness play in the process of manifestation, and how can we overcome limiting beliefs to truly live as conscious creators?"*

There was no immediate answer. Only the low hum of the wind whispering through the neem trees outside, and the occasional flutter of a moth drawn to the spiritual flame.

Guruji looked toward Roopa. His eyes held a gaze not of pity, but of deep knowing. He gently placed his palm over his heart.

"Roopa," he said, "fear is not your enemy. It is your *threshold*."

He let the silence stretch like the edge of a cliff.

"Fear is the guardian standing before the door of transformation. It asks not to be banished, but to be *understood*. To live as a conscious creator is not to be free of fear—it is to walk with it, lovingly, until it no longer leads the way."

He paused and gestured to the flame in the corner.

"Do you see that, Jyoti? It flickers not because it is weak, but because it dances with the wind and *remains lit*. That, Roopa, is fearlessness—not the absence of fear, but the presence of unwavering light."

### The Weaver Who Feared the Sky

Guruji said, "Karthik was a gifted weaver in a village of Kanchipuram. His hands could create patterns no one had ever seen—saris that shimmered like dawn, shawls that whispered of monsoon rains.

But he lived in a hut with a low roof. Always hunched, always confined.

You see, Karthik feared the sky.

Not storms. Not lightning.

He feared *vastness*.

As a child, he was told, *"Don't dream too big—you'll fall. Stay low. Stay safe."* And so, even when buyers came offering fortunes, Karthik refused.

"I am just a village weaver," he would say. "My loom belongs to the ground."

One year, after much persuasion, he agreed to visit the ashram. He sat quietly at the back, never speaking, always watching. Until one day, during a satsang on liberation, he whispered to Guruji after everyone had left:

"What if I am meant for more… but the voice in me says I will fail?"

Guruji smiled gently and gave him a task.

"Weave a tapestry," he said. "But not with your hands. With your fears. Every day, write down one fear that limits you. Then, beside it, write what you would do if that fear were not true."

Karthik did this for 21 days.

"I fear I'm not worthy."

## THE POWER OF MANIFESTATION

*If this weren't true, I'd send my work to Chennai (City).*

"I fear I'll disappoint my family."

*If this weren't true, I'd teach children how to weave beauty from pain.*

By the end of three weeks, he had pages filled with dreams woven through shadows.

Then Guruji handed him a matchstick and said:

"Let the past burn, and offer its ash to the wind. Now go… weave the sky."

Karthik left the ashram and built a studio with an open roof. His first new sari was called *"Antariksha"*—*Sky Without Walls.*

Today, his looms sing stories of freedom. Not because fear disappeared, but because he *no longer believed it more than he believed in himself.*

Back in Shambav Hall, Guruji looked back at Roopa.

"You asked about manifestation. But manifestation is not just about what you want—it is about *who you're willing to become* to receive it."

Guruji rose slowly, his robes catching the golden shimmer of the lamp's light.

"If you carry fear like a weight, it will anchor your dreams to the ground. But if you carry it like a compass, it will point to the exact belief you must outgrow."

He walked toward the flame, now gently swaying.

"You are not here to repeat old stories. You are here to write new ones—with courage as your ink and freedom as your page."

Guruji said, "The universe responds not to who you pretend to be, but to who you *dare to become* when no one else is watching."

And just then, a soft breeze entered the hall through the open window. The flame flickered once more—but did not go out.

It danced.

# WRAP UP

## Becoming the Architect of Your Destiny

*"To become the architect of your destiny, you must first align with the flow of the universe. The power lies not in the struggle, but in the surrender to the cosmic rhythm that guides your soul."*

– Shree Shambav

### Synopsis:

This invites readers to awaken to their true essence as conscious creators. It emphasises that life is not about striving with force, but about aligning with the natural rhythm of the universe. When the heart, mind, and soul move in harmony with this greater intelligence, manifestation becomes an unfolding rather than a struggle. You are not a passive receiver of circumstances, but a powerful architect of your destiny—one who shapes reality by tuning into the sacred current of intention, trust, and co-creation. This is a gentle but powerful reminder: the more you align, the less you need to chase. Your dreams begin to find you.

Padma, with a soft reverence in her eyes, leaned slightly forward and asked, "Guruji, how does alignment with the universe differ from forcing our desires, and why is it the key to becoming the architect of our own destiny?"

Guruji began slowly, "Padma, have you ever seen a river that tries to climb uphill?"

She shook her head gently.

"That is what forcing desires looks like," he said. "You can try to build dams, divert currents, or command the water to rise—but it resists, because its nature is flow. Now think of a boatman who learns to read the river's rhythm. He listens. He waits. He aligns his oars with the current, and in doing so, he travels farther with less effort. This is alignment."

The devotees listened in complete silence. Guruji's words echoed not just in the air, but in the stillness of their hearts.

"To force," Guruji continued, "is to act from fear. From the illusion that the universe is against you. From the belief that you must wrestle with reality to shape your fate. But alignment is trust. It is surrender without passivity, effort without tension. It is the art of listening to the signs, the whispers of intuition, the nudges of synchronicity."

He paused and looked at Padma, "Years ago," he said, "a man named Vikram came to me, anxious and burnt out. He had a dream to build a school in his village, but every door he knocked on remained closed. He blamed fate, he blamed people, and he blamed himself. He worked tirelessly but joylessly, driven by the fear of failure. His dream was noble, but his approach was soaked in resistance. He wanted the flower to bloom by pulling at its petals.

One afternoon, I gave him a different task. I asked him to plant a seed, water it daily, but do nothing else. No digging. No checking. No doubting. Just presence. Just care.

He returned a few months later, changed.

'I stopped trying to prove anything, Guruji,' he said. 'I started listening more than pushing. And when I stopped demanding the dream to appear on my timeline, people began offering help. Unexpected donors showed up. Land was gifted. I simply became the steward of the dream, not its controller.'

That school now teaches over two hundred children.

Guruji smiled. "This is the power of alignment. When you harmonise your thoughts, emotions, and actions with the frequency of your deepest truth, the universe no longer resists you—because you are no longer resisting it."

He looked around the hall.

"When you force, you are saying: 'I don't trust.' When you align, you say: 'I am ready.' And when readiness meets divine timing, destiny unfolds like the petals of a lotus—gracefully, naturally, inevitably."

Padma's eyes glistened. Something unspoken inside her had softened.

Guruji said, "To be the architect of your destiny, you must first become the architect of your inner space. For it is not willpower but inner alignment that draws the blueprint of miracles."

*Akshaya, sitting with a stillness that spoke of something deeper stirring within, gently asked, "Guruji, what role does trust play in the process of co-creation, and how can we learn to trust the universe in shaping our path?"*

Guruji closed his eyes briefly, and when he opened them, they shimmered with a calm knowingness. He looked at Akshaya, then at the flame, and said, "Trust, Akshaya, is not just a belief—it is the soul's posture. It is the silence between the breath, the surrender in the pause before action. Without trust, co-creation becomes a negotiation. With trust, it becomes a dance."

"Many years ago," Guruji said, "there lived a sculptor named Mohan in a village nestled by the hills. He was renowned for his skill, but his heart was often heavy with doubt. Every block of stone he touched, he questioned: *Will this turn out right? Will the form reveal itself? Will I fail?*

One day, after a storm had swept through the village, a large rock was dislodged and landed near the temple. The villagers asked Mohan to sculpt something divine from it. But when he examined the stone, he hesitated.

'This one's too flawed,' he muttered. 'It has cracks, too many impurities.'

But an old woman, who had always admired his work, said softly, 'Mohan, the stone did not roll here by accident. Perhaps it chose *you*. Can you not trust that?'

Her words stayed with him.

For weeks, he sat by the rock—not chiselling, not carving, but simply observing. He began to feel its contours, its hidden strength, its silent whispers. One morning, without overthinking, he picked up his chisel and began sculpting—not from fear or perfectionism, but from trust. Stroke by stroke, guided not by his mind, but by a deeper knowing, the form revealed itself.

Months later, when he was done, the statue of the goddess that emerged was unlike any he had ever created. Devotees wept before it. Even Raghav, when he looked into her eyes, felt as though she had been waiting inside that flawed stone all along—for his trust to set her free."

Guruji looked around at the devotees, then back at Akshaya.

"You see," he said, "trust is not blind. It is the deepest form of vision—the kind that sees *through* the obstacle to the invitation behind it. When we trust the universe, we are saying: *I believe there is a higher order, even if I cannot yet perceive it.* Co-creation does not mean control. It means collaboration with a wisdom larger than your own."

Akshaya nodded slowly, his eyes misting.

"But Guruji," he asked softly, "how do we learn to trust when the path feels unclear?"

Guruji smiled, "You begin by remembering. Every breath you take happens without your instruction. Your heart beats, your cells renew, your wounds close—not because you force them, but because Life knows how to carry you. If it has carried you this far, why would it abandon you now?"

He continued, "Trust begins in small acts—listening to your intuition, honouring synchronicities, releasing what is no longer meant for you, and most of all, staying open when your mind craves answers. The universe is not late. It is deliberate."

Then, gently, Guruji said, "Imagine you are planting a seed. You do not dig it up every day to see if it's growing. You water it, give it sunlight, protect it—and most importantly, *you trust the process*. That trust is what allows the unseen to become seen."

The flame beside him flickered again, not wildly, but as if in gentle agreement. And in that moment, Shambav Hall felt less like a building, and more like the heart of the universe breathing—in trust, in surrender, in sacred co-creation.

Guruji sat still for a long time, his eyes half-closed, as though listening not to the world around him, but to something ancient and vast within. The silence in Shambav Hall was alive—charged, sacred. Every soul present seemed to feel the same breathless hush, like the space between the final note of a symphony and its echo.

And then, gently—almost imperceptibly—Guruji rose from his asana.

He didn't speak at first. He simply stood, palms folded, eyes soft with compassion and completeness. Slowly, with a serene dignity, he began to walk down the centre of the hall. The flicker of the divine flame in the corner—Lakshmi Vilakku—cast golden shadows upon the walls, dancing in rhythm with the reverence in everyone's hearts.

One by one, the devotees rose. No words were exchanged. They bowed, some with folded hands, some with eyes brimming with unshed tears. The kind of tears that come not from sorrow, but from the fullness of being seen, of having touched something real.

And with that silent farewell, the retreat was concluded.

Outside, the night had descended gently, like a mother laying a blanket over her children. The sky was a vast canvas—deep indigo, adorned with stars shimmering like ancient witnesses. The breeze was cool and fragrant with sandalwood and jasmine. Trees swayed softly, as if bowing to an invisible raga playing somewhere in the sky. Crickets sang their hymn to the night, and the wind carried whispers of the day just passed.

Rohith, Sujitha, and a few others lingered near the threshold of Shambav Hall, reluctant to leave the sacred space just yet. Eventually, they made their way to the dining area, and after a quiet, reflective dinner and a few moments of refreshing themselves, they gravitated toward the fireplace—their unofficial gathering place.

The fire crackled gently, flames dancing like old storytellers sharing secrets with the stars.

Espen, Astyn, Kieron, Martina, and Greta were already seated, huddled close, their voices low and reverent, still echoing the themes of the day. Their faces glowed with both firelight and the light of inner discovery. Soon, Akshaya, Vasudeva, and a few others joined, forming a circle of warmth and memory.

Astyn turned, a gentle urgency in her voice. "Apeksha, we've been waiting… We need to hear something from you—one last story to carry home."

Apeksha smiled softly. Her eyes reflected both the firelight and the wisdom she had gathered over years of listening—not just to words, but to silences. She took a moment, letting the stillness ripen.

Then she spoke.

"There was once a young man who came to Guruji, desperate and disillusioned," Apeksha began, her voice smooth as moonlight. "He had been manifesting with discipline—vision boards, journaling, affirmations—but nothing was working. *Nothing*. His frustration had become louder than his faith."

She paused, letting the moment breathe.

"Guruji didn't lecture. He simply gave him a lamp—unlit—and said, 'Take this to the riverbank and sit with it each night, without lighting it, until you understand the darkness.'"

Apeksha's eyes glistened. "For weeks, the young man sat by the water, confused and angry. But slowly, the silence taught him. He began to see how much fear he carried, how much of his manifesting came not from trust, but from lack—from the fear that he was not enough. And then one night, as stars bloomed above him and the river hummed softly, he finally understood. He struck the match and lit the lamp—not for the outcome, but for the peace of knowing he was no longer hiding from the dark within himself. That night, he became the light."

A hush fell over the circle. Even the wind seemed to be still.

Apeksha continued, her tone even softer now. "And then, there was the story of Meena—a woman who had lost everything. A business, a relationship, even her sense of self. She came to the retreat not to learn, but simply to escape. But Guruji saw through her silence. During a nature walk, he picked up a fallen leaf—brown, dry, forgotten. He handed it to her and said, 'Even this was once green. Even this danced in the wind. And now, it returns to the soil, not as loss, but as part of something greater.'

Meena kept that leaf with her. It became her talisman. Not long after, she started painting again—something she hadn't done since childhood. What she lost didn't return, but what she found was something more sacred: herself."

The fire crackled once more, casting long shadows. The stars above seemed to lean in, listening.

Kiran stretched and sighed, "It's time to rest. Tomorrow morning, we all return to the world that awaits."

There was a pause. A sacred reluctance.

Lalith smiled wistfully, "The retreat passed like a sigh. I learned more in these days than I have in years."

"I feel that too," Sujitha nodded. "Like something inside me has shifted… quietly, but forever."

Rohith added, "We came searching, but we leave remembering."

One by one, they each offered their reflections. No one wanted to say goodbye, not really. Because it didn't feel like the end—it felt like a soft, sacred beginning.

The fire dimmed, the sky deepened, and sleep began calling them gently home.

As they dispersed into the night, feet brushing the dewy grass and hearts quietly full, the final words seemed to echo from the stars themselves:

**"The retreat has ended… but the journey continues."**

# The Garden Within

A question rose—not loud, but deep—
From lips once sealed by silent grief:
"How can I feel what I long to be,
When shadows breathe so close to me?"

No answer broke the quiet air,
But hush became a sacred prayer.
In stillness vast and undefined,
The soul began to gently find—

"To shape the world, begin within,
Where feelings root, and truths begin.
It's not the mind alone that steers,
But hearts aligned beyond the fears."

The inner earth must first be turned,
With tenderness the soul has earned.

For seeds of dreams refuse to rise
Where rage still burns and sorrow lies.

You cannot wish with trembling breath,
Or summon life while fearing death.
A thousand thoughts may sing your song,
But feeling keeps the rhythm strong.

There lived a soul who chased the skies,
With maps of stars and fierce replies.
Yet stars stayed veiled, the skies withdrew—
For what he thought, he never knew.

His mind was sharp, his goals were bright,
But the heart was dimmed, eclipsed by night.
And fate, like time, stood still and wise—
Not to deny, but crystallise.

Then came a dawn—no fire, no storm—
Just quiet ache, a shifting form.
He chose to feel, not to escape—
He sat within his own heart's ache.

## THE POWER OF MANIFESTATION

He wept, he shook, he met the shade,
Where all his ghosts in silence laid.
And in that space where pain was seen,
The tender roots of joy grew green.

"To manifest," the soul then knew,
"Is not to chase what's not yet true.
But be the spring, the fertile ground,
Where peace and purpose both are found."

"To dream is not to plead or strive,
But breathe as if the dream's alive.
Let gratitude precede the gain—
That is the key that ends the chain."

So if you seek to shift your fate,
Begin not late, nor complicate.
Begin with breath, with grace, with pause—
Let love, not lack, become your cause.

For when emotion flows as one
With thought, with truth, with setting sun—

The world bends gently to your call,
And dreams, like blossoms, start to fall.

# Life Coach and Philanthropist

Shree Shambav is the visionary founder of the Shree Shambav Ayur Rakshita Foundation (www.shambav-ayurrakshita.org). He founded this institution with a lofty goal: to recognise human identity across gender, ethnicity, and nationality. Through this organisation, he wants to assist all communities in realising their full potential and the intrinsic beauty of life.

Shree Shambav, a Life Coach, is dedicated to supporting people on their journeys of self-discovery and empowerment. He assists people in discovering who they are, determining what inspires and drives them, and overcoming limiting ideas. His approach clarifies what one wants in life, assisting people through goal-setting and a step-by-step process for achieving them. He empowers people to make deliberate and responsible decisions, allowing them to identify their blind spots and evolve as individuals via the use of numerous strategies and tools.

The foundation's bold, uncompromising, and compassionate ventures are always aimed at initiating the "Inner Transformation" process. They focus on spiritual growth, personal growth, and self-healing while emphasising that true progress lies in "Inclusive Growth and Co-existence." This philosophy drives all their initiatives, encouraging a holistic approach to development and well-being.

Under Shree Shambav's leadership, the foundation has launched several impactful movements:

Shree Shambav Green Movement: This mission is to create a healthy, green, and clean earth through responsible water conservation and greening initiatives. The movement strives to make the world a green paradise by encouraging sustainable living and environmental responsibility.

Shree Shambav Vidya Vedhika (Vizhuthugal): This project aims to help students and children by offering training, books, stationery, and uniforms. It aims to provide the next generation with the tools and resources they need to excel both academically and personally.

Shree Shambav and his foundation exemplify the spirit of compassion, transformation, and inclusive growth via their work, which has a profound impact on individuals and communities around the world. His work exemplifies the power of acknowledging and nourishing the human spirit, creating a world in which everyone can reach their full potential and appreciate the beauty of life.

# TESTIMONIALS

**Journey of Soul - Karma** - "We die in our twenties and are buried at eighty." Remember that nothing can stop someone who refuses to be stopped. "Most people do not fail; they simply give up." Shree Shambav deserves full credit. It allowed me to sit and consider what I might miss out on in life. The author has delved into every aspect of our daily lives. How can a seemingly insignificant change in these seemingly insignificant details bring us such joy? The Soul of Journey teaches you the "art of living" as well as the "art of dying."

**Twenty + One Series** - The rich cultural heritage offered a host of twenty + one short stories with incredible imagination, morals and values prevalent at a given time, influencing how people respond to a crisis or any situation. The author has recreated images with universal values and morals. The plethora of fascinating stories from faraway lands would leave the modern play and story writers a cringe. The book supports trust and immeasurable values, instilling hope for the new generations.

**Death** - "Shree Shambav's 'Death - Light of Life and the Shadow of Death' is an extraordinary masterpiece that delves deep into the profound questions surrounding our existence and mortality. The book's opening statement, 'Nothing ever truly dies; it simply ceases to exist in one form before resuming it in another,' sets the stage for a thought-provoking exploration of death's multifaceted nature. Shambav's remarkable ability to navigate the philosophical complexities of death and our universal fear of it is both enlightening and comforting. This book is a testament to the power of understanding and acceptance."

**Whispers of Eternity** - "Reading 'Whispers of Eternity' by Shree Shambav was a transformative experience that left me captivated from beginning to end. Each section of this exquisite collection delves into the myriad facets of existence, offering poignant reflections on life, death, and everything in between. Shree Shambav's verses are a testament to the beauty of language and the power of expression, inviting readers to embark on a journey of self-discovery and spiritual awakening. Whether celebrating life's simple joys or grappling with the complexities of human emotion, this book is a timeless companion that speaks to the heart and soul of every reader."

**Life Changing Journey Series** - "Life Changing Journey Series II Inspirational Quotes" is a remarkable collection that illuminates the path to self-discovery and personal growth. With its inspiring quotes and insightful reflections, this book serves as a beacon of light in a world often shrouded in darkness. Each quote offers wisdom, guidance, and encouragement, reminding readers of their inner strength and resilience. A must-read for anyone seeking inspiration and enlightenment.

**Learn To Love Yourself –** "A Heartfelt Guide to Authentic Self-Love." "Learn to Love Yourself" invites readers on a transformative journey to embrace their true essence in a world often focused on external validation. Through ten insightful chapters, it gently reveals principles of genuine self-love, guiding readers to deepen their connection with themselves. Beyond surface positivity, it encourages the cultivation of resilient self-acceptance, from embracing one's unique qualities to setting empowering boundaries. With inspiring stories and practical wisdom, this book is a trusted companion on the path to inner peace, fulfilment, and joy, helping readers build lives that reflect their authentic selves.

**The Power of Letting Go** – This book has been a gift to my spiritual journey. Shree Shambav's insights into attachment, personal growth cycles, and forgiveness are enlightening. The concept of seven-year cycles resonated with me, helping me understand the natural phases of life. I feel more empowered to let go of what no longer serves me and step into a life of freedom and fulfilment. A truly beautiful read!

**A Journey of Lasting Peace** – "A Journey of Lasting Peace" feels like a trusted friend guiding you through the maze of self-discovery. The 18 transformative principles are both practical and deeply resonant, addressing everything from gratitude practices to the art of letting go. Each chapter is infused with warmth and wisdom, making it easy to apply the concepts to my life. I particularly appreciated the emphasis on physical health's connection to mental well-being; it served as a wake-up call for me to prioritise my health. This book is an invaluable resource for anyone serious about personal growth!

**Astrology Unveiled Series** – "Profound, Logical, and Inspiring". What stands out in Astrology Unveiled is the author's dedication to making Vedic astrology logical and approachable. Each concept flows naturally into the next, backed by examples and exercises. The insights into karma and life cycles add a philosophical depth rarely seen in astrology books. Perfect for anyone seeking spiritual growth alongside astrological knowledge!

**The Entitlement Trap -** "Thought-Provoking and Challenging" The book challenges readers to confront their own sense of entitlement, and that's not easy—but it's essential. The Entitlement Trap doesn't offer a one-size-fits-all approach. Instead, it's a thoughtful, layered examination of how entitlement can limit our growth. The chapter on "Defining Your Own Hill" was particularly impactful, as it pushed me to reconsider which challenges are truly worth pursuing. A thought-provoking read for those willing to do the inner work to create a life they can be proud of.

**Whispers of a Dying Soul** – "A Soul-Stirring Reflection on Life's Unspoken Truths" **-** *Whispers of a Dying Soul: Unspoken Regrets and Unlived Dreams"* is a deeply moving exploration of the unexpressed emotions and unfulfilled aspirations that shape our lives in ways we often don't realise. This book invites readers to confront the powerful, often hidden impact of regret while guiding them through a journey of introspection and healing. Each page opens a space to reflect on the choices that define us—from moments of unspoken love to neglected passions—offering a gentle reminder to live authentically and courageously.

**Whispers of the Soul: A Journey Through Haiku -** is a mesmerising collection that speaks directly to the heart. Each haiku is a delicate brushstroke capturing life's fleeting beauty and timeless wisdom, inviting readers into moments of deep reflection and peace. This book is a balm for the soul, guiding us to find meaning in stillness and connection in simplicity. The themes of nature, love, and mindfulness echo universal truths, resonating with quiet, powerful grace. It's a book to be savoured slowly, cherished deeply, and returned to often. Truly, a gift for anyone seeking calm and clarity in life's chaos.

**Whispers of Silence** - Unlocking Inner Power through Stillness by Shree Shambav is a rare gem that beckons readers to pause, reflect, and reconnect with their inner selves. In a world that never stops talking, this book offers a profound exploration of silence—not as a void but as a rich and transformative space.

From the first page, Shree Shambav's writing resonates deeply, blending scientific insights with spiritual wisdom in a way that feels both universal and deeply personal. The author's ability to bridge the tangible and the transcendent makes this book an invaluable guide for anyone navigating the chaos of modern life.

**The Power of Words: Transforming Speech, Transforming Lives** - "The Power of Words is a profound and enlightening guide that has transformed the way I approach communication. Shree Shambav masterfully uncovers the hidden influence of our words on relationships, self-perception, and overall well-being. This book doesn't just teach you how to speak; it inspires mindful communication that fosters connection and trust. The insights on replacing negative patterns like gossip and judgment with kindness and authenticity are truly life-changing. The practical strategies and engaging narratives make it an invaluable resource for personal and professional growth. A must-read for anyone striving to communicate with intention, clarity, and compassion. Highly recommended!"

**The Art of Intentional Living: Minimalism for a Life of Purpose -** "The Art of Intentional Living is a refreshing guide to finding clarity in a cluttered world. With practical wisdom and profound insights, it inspires you to simplify, prioritise, and live with purpose. A must-read for anyone seeking balance and fulfilment."

**Awakening the Infinite: The Power of Consciousness in Transforming Life -** "Awakening the Infinite is a transformative guide that expands the mind and nourishes the soul. With profound insights and practical wisdom, this book beautifully explores the power of consciousness, helping readers connect with their true purpose and inner potential. It is a journey of self-discovery, healing, and spiritual awakening, offering clarity and inspiration at every turn. A must-read for anyone looking to live with greater awareness, meaning, and authenticity."

**Beyond the Veil: A Journey Through Life After Death:**

"This book touched me in ways few others have—it's not just about death, but about life, meaning, and the vast unknown that connects them. Beyond the Veil offers a graceful blend of science and spirit, inviting us to explore the mystery with awe rather than fear. The stories, insights, and reflections linger in your heart long after the final page. A truly transformative read that brings light to the shadows of mortality. It reminded me that in embracing death, we truly learn how to live."

**Bonds Beyond Blood:**

"A profoundly moving story that reminds us family is not defined by blood, but by love, sacrifice, and the courage to heal. Every chapter touched my soul with its emotional truth and timeless wisdom. Through joy, grief, and redemption, this book captures the raw beauty of human connection. I saw reflections of my own family in its pages—both the pain and the hope. A powerful, unforgettable read that lingers long after the final word."

**A Journey into Spiritual Maturity: 12 Golden Rules for Inner Transformation**

"This book is a gentle yet powerful guide that awakened a deeper sense of purpose within me. Each golden rule felt like a mirror reflecting truths I needed to embrace. Shree Shambav's wisdom is timeless, poetic, and profoundly grounding. It's not just a read—it's a journey into the heart of who you truly are. A must-read for anyone seeking lasting peace, clarity, and inner transformation."

**The Inner Battlefield: Overcoming the Enemies of the Mind and Soul:**

"This book is a powerful revelation—an honest mirror to the battles we fight within. Every chapter is a step closer to clarity, peace, and emotional mastery. Shree Shambav brilliantly transforms ancient wisdom into practical guidance for modern souls. It awakened in me a new strength to face my fears and rise above inner turmoil. A must-read for anyone seeking true inner victory and lasting transformation."

## The Seeker's Gold – Unlocking Life's Greatest Treasure

*The Seeker's Gold* is a soul-stirring masterpiece that goes far beyond the pursuit of wealth—it is a journey into the heart of what truly matters. Each chapter unfolds with poetic wisdom and emotional depth, revealing that life's real treasure is not found in riches but in the transformation of the self. As the protagonist evolves through trials, love, and profound realizations, so does the reader. This book is a mirror for every dreamer, a lantern for every seeker, and a companion for anyone walking the path of purpose. A timeless tale that stays with you long after the final page.

# ACKNOWLEDGEMENTS

To my grandfathers, grandmothers, mothers, fathers, aunts, uncles, neighbours, sisters, brothers, friends, and teachers, they poured in endless moral stories, retellings of Ramayana, Mahabharata, Puranas, Upanishads, and so on.

My teachers, neighbours, and kindred souls. Who provided us with a stage to perform wonderful Puranic stories and were gracious enough to acknowledge our efforts.

The artists and translators of epics have served as a source of inspiration, invigorating our spirits, making these works accessible, and enabling us to grasp the profound depths and deeper dimensions they contain.

I also cherish the stimulating conversations; I had with my wonderful mothers, Punitha Muniswamy and Uma Devi.

Our family's youngest member, Aadhya, who always overwhelmed me with questions, inspired this book.

I would likewise prefer to express gratitude to Mr Sivakumar, Mrs Roopa Sivakumar, Mr Akshaya Rajesh, Ms Akshatha Rajesh, Ms Apeksha Prabhu, Mr Akanksh Prabhu, Mr Nikash Sarasambi, and Mrs Spoorthi Nikash for their valuable inputs.

I must thank Mr Rajesh, Mr Savan Prabhu, Mrs Revathi Rajesh, Mrs Rajani Sarasambi, and Mrs Manju Reshma, who encouraged me and often suggested writing a book. Their unwavering belief that I had something valuable to offer kept me going during my writing sessions.

Love you all,

**Shree Shambav**

www.shambav.org

shreeshambav@gmail.com

www.ingramcontent.com/pod-product-compliance
Lightning Source LLC
LaVergne TN
LVHW091540070526
838199LV00002B/140